Violet Island
and Other *Poems*

GREEN INTEGER BOOKS
Edited by Per Bregne
København / Los Angeles

Distributed in the United States by Consortium Book
Sales and Distribution, 1045 Westgate Drive, Suite 90,
Saint Paul, Minnesota 55114-1065
Distributed in England and throughout Europe by
Turnaround Publisher Services, Unit 3, Olympia Trading Estate,
Coburg Road, Wood Green, London N22 6TZ
44 (0)20 88293009

(323) 857-1115 / http://www.greeninteger.com

First Green Integer Edition 2004
English language copyright ©2004
by Kristin Dykstra and Nancy Gates Madsen
Afterword ©2004 by Kristin Dykstra
Poems in this volume were selected from five volumes of poetry
published in Cuba: *Cuando una mujer no duerme* (Havana:
Ediciones Unión, 1982); *Para un cordero blanco* (Havana: Casa de
las Américas, 1984); *En la arena de Padua* (Havana: Ediciones
Unión, 1992); *Páramos* (Havana: Ediciones Unión, 1995); and
La foto del invernadero (Havana: Casa de las Américas, 1998)
©1998, 1995, 1992, 1984, and 1982 by Reina María Rodríguez
Printed by agreement with Reina María Rodríguez
Back cover copy ©2004 by Green Integer
All rights reserved.
This book was made possible, in part, through grants from
the English Department and the College of Arts & Sciences
at Illinois State University

Design: Per Bregne
Typography & Cover: Trudy Fisher
Cover Photograph: Reina María Rodríguez by Enzo Aneiros

LIBRARY OF CONGRESS CATALOGING IN PUBLICATION DATA
Reina María Rodríguez [1952]
Violet Island and Other Poems
ISBN: 1-892295-65-2
p. cm — Green Integer 119
I. Title II. Series III. Translator

Green Integer books are published for Douglas Messerli
Printed in the United States on acid-free paper.

Reina María Rodríguez

Violet Island and Other *Poems*

Translated from the Spanish
by Kristin Dykstra and Nancy Gates Madsen

GREEN INTEGER
KØBENHAVN & LOS ANGELES
2004

contents

deudas

hoy quisiera escribir lo que me falta
no gastar las horas
ni echar palabras al abismo:
bajar a mis profundidades
sola y desnuda.
qué pruebas puedo dar de mi mortalidad?
soy sencillamente fea
con pecas, sueños y dolores.
tengo dos hijos
otro que nacerá el próximo septiembre.
no soy un buen negocio
— enseguida salgo embarazada —.
soy el número 338 123 del carnet de identidad
sin foto — los niños la rompieron —
ni sanción — porque no poseo antecedentes penales
mayores ni menores —
trabajo como redactora de programas
un sueldo de 163 pesos
una literatura de carrera
muchos poemas sueltos
y amigos en cuatro categorías:
regulares buenos muy malos y tristes.
una casa ajena
un ventilador, un peine
la balalaica que me trajo mi hermano
el piano de los conciertos infantiles
una lupa para ver mejor la realidad

debts

today I want to write about what I'm missing
not to waste hours
or to throw words into the abyss:
to sink into my depths
alone and naked.
what proof can I give of my mortality?
I'm just plain
with freckles, dreams and sorrow.
I have two children
another will be born in September.
I'm a bad lay
— I get pregnant just like that —
I'm number 338123 on my identity card
no photo — the kids ripped it up —
no record of offenses,
serious or petty —
I work as a program editor
a salary of 163 pesos
a literature degree
many uncollected poems
and friends in four categories:
reliable   good   terrible and sad.
a house that isn't mine
an electric fan, a comb
the balalaika that my brother brought me
the piano from childhood concerts
a magnifying glass to see reality better

las fotos de Martí y Hemingway
reproducciones
libros que aún no me han robado
mapas ampliando la pared
cartas de antiguos amantes
un reloj, una mariposa azul, un corazón
y muchas deudas
infinitas deudas con la vida.

photos of Martí and Hemingway
reproductions
books they haven't stolen from me yet
maps widening the wall
letters from old lovers
a watch, a blue butterfly, a heart
and many debts
infinite debts with life.

remordimientos para un cordero
blanco

no me puedo librar de ese ojo
que mira desde el cuadro
mis imperfecciones.
toda mi culpa de vivir
y querer
invitándome.
me estoy buscando
y tengo miedo
casi un miedo fanático
de haber sido cómplice
inacabada
porque también sonreí cuando quería matar.
mis mentiras son sueños
agua que no nadé
y este vicio
este vicio de mariposas
un solo día volando sin cesar
luego polvillo oscuro sobre las violetas.
perdóname, ojo de mi cordero adolescente
si en estos años te engañé
y pude ser
diferente.

remorse for a white lamb

I can't free myself from the eye
it watches my imperfections
from a painting.
all my guilt of living
and wanting
invites me.
I'm searching for myself
and I'm afraid
almost fanatically afraid
of having been an accomplice
unfinished
because I also smiled when I wanted to kill.
my lies are dreams
water I didn't swim
and this vice
this butterfly vice
one single day of continuous flight
then a fine dark dust on violets.
forgive me, eye of my adolescent lamb
if in these years I deceived you
and I could have been
different.

las islas

mira y no les descuides.
las islas son mundos aparentes.
cortadas en el mar
transcurren en su soledad de tierras sin raíz.
en el silencio del agua una mancha
de haber anclado sólo aquella vez
y poner los despojos de la tempestad y las ráfagas
sobre las olas.
aquí los cementerios son hermosos y pequeños
y están más allá de las ceremonias.
me he bañado para sentarme en la yerba
es la zona de brumas
donde acontecen los espejismos
y vuelvo a sonreír.
no sé si estás aquí o es el peligro
empiezo a ser libre entre esos límites que se
    intercambian:
seguro amanecerá.
las islas son mundos aparentes
coberturas del cansancio en los iniciadores de la calma
sé que sólo en mí estuvo aquella vez la realidad
un intervalo entre dos tiempos
cortadas en el mar
soy lanzada hacia un lugar más tenue
las muchachas que serán jóvenes una vez más
contra la sabiduria y la rigidez de los que envejecieron

the islands

look and don't neglect them.
the islands are apparent worlds.
cut off in the sea
moving past in the solitude of rootless lands.
above the water's silence, a stain
from having dropped anchor only that once
depositing remains left by storms and gusts
on the waves.
here the cemeteries are beautiful and small.
they are beyond ceremonies.
I bathed before sitting down in the grass
it's the zone of thick sea mists
where mirages occur
and I smile again.
I don't know if you're here or if it's the danger
I begin to be free between those interchanging limits:
surely dawn will come.
the islands are apparent worlds
blankets of exhaustion on those who would bring about
    calm
I know the reality was only inside me then
an interval between two kinds of time
cut off in the sea
I'm thrown onto a more tenuous place
girls who will be young one more time
in the face of the wisdom and the rigidity of those who
    aged

sin los movimientos y las contorsiones del mar
las islas son mundos aparentes manchas de sal
otra mujer lanzada encima de mí que no conozco
sólo la vida menor
la gratitud sin prisa de las islas en mí.

without the motions and contortions of the sea
the islands are apparent worlds   salt stains
another woman I don't know, thrown on top of me
only the lesser life
the unhurried gratitude of the islands in me.

fin de año: se busca

(entre Ana Frank y yo)
— pues lo que te pregunto es si has visto el mundo.
— pues . . . lo que se dice verlo . . .
es que no pude encontrarlo . . .
— Ana Frank, 23 de abril de 1944

el día se pierde y envejezco.
detrás de este día estamos perdidos.
pasamos largas filas de escombros
largas filas de caras cóncavas.
no puedo levantar la cabeza ni las piernas
tengo angustia
con su saco gris aplastándome.
debe ser una mala jugada
con su martillo quiere comprender y dar
su último golpe.
si pudiera llegar hasta aquella claridad.
se enciende a lo lejos la luz de una lámpara.
yo también he vivido como tú
la niña que presintió el incendio.
si pudiera llegar.
sé que no podré ser la misma
no puedo ser otro animal y dejar a mi propio
ser humano en el pasado.
estoy vestida de negro y aunque no lo parezca
soy judía   ustedes no lo sospechan
vivo en una tierra extraña en un mundo extraño

year's end: wanted

(between Anne Frank and me)
— what I'm asking you is whether you've seen the world.
— well . . . what you call seeing the world . . .
it's just that I couldn't find it . . .
— Anne Frank, April 23, 1944

the day dissolves and I grow old.
behind this day we're lost
we pass long rows of debris
long rows of concave faces.
I can't lift my head or my legs
suffering
crushes me, gray suit-jacket.
it must be a bad move in the game,
wants to understand like a hammer,
to strike a final blow.
if I could get to that clarity.
a lamplight goes on in the distance.
I too have lived like you
the girl who foresaw the fire.
if I could get there.
I know I won't be able to stay the same
I can't be another animal and leave my own
human self in the past.
I'm dressed in black and although I don't look it
I am a jew   none of you suspect it
I live in a strange land in a strange world

y me persiguen.
quisiera romper la percepción ordinaria
porque no vivo en el lugar que me han descrito
del que sólo poseo una señal no una idea.
tienen ustedes una idea de la curvatura terrestre
cuando me amarro los zapatos?
pensando algunas veces en dios
en mi pequeño dios individual
digo alguna que otra verdad
se busca: dice un cartel y me azoro.
afuera preparan otro modo de estar
alquilan cuartos pintan las paredes se habitúan.
el estar en revolución adentro es menos aparente
a esta fachada que se deteriora.
somos espectadores pacientes
imitadores soñadores de una realidad.
soterrada en medio del tedio
me tomo equivocada la vida
tengo 13 años
pasará el veneno y mi corazón estará alegre?
no quiero defenderme
la alegría no tiene conexión con la defensa.
mi mamá sube y baja los escalones del sótano
carga agua
aquí donde me escondo carecemos de muchas cosas
pero acariciaremos a las plantas?

and they hound me.
I'd like to break with normal perception
because I don't live in the place that they've described to
 me
a place of which I have only a sign, not an idea.
do you have any idea of how the earth curves
when I'm tying my shoes?
thinking sometimes of god
of my small individual god
I speak some truth or another
wanted: says a poster, and I get nervous.
outside they prepare another mode of being
they rent rooms   they paint the walls   they get used to
 things.
being in inner revolution is less apparent
to this deteriorating façade.
we are patient spectators
imitators   dreamers of a reality.
buried in tedium
I take life the wrong way
I'm thirteen
will this poison pass and my heart be happy?
I don't want to defend myself
happiness has no connection to defense.
my mother goes up and down the basement stairs
she carries water
here where I hide myself we lack many things
but will we reach down for those plants?

desarrollaremos toda la sensibilidad de la especie?
algunos tienen miedo del fondo
y nadan boca arriba para no verlas
pero ellas están ahí nada más
las plantas que esperan ser acariciadas.
será el final de la pareja humana?
tengo 13 años
y estoy soterrada
podremos cambiar la superficie sin miedo
a bucear y que nos enreden las plantas
benévolas y terribles del fondo?
estoy vestida de gris y aunque no lo parezca
tengo cientos de años
ustedes no lo saben no los sopechan
vivo en una tierra extraña en un mundo extraño
y me persiguen.

will we develop all the sensibility of the species?
some are afraid of the depths
and swim face up so as not to see them
but they are simply there
plants, waiting to be stroked.
will it be the end of human coupling?
I'm thirteen
and I'm underground
will we be able to change the surface without fear,
dive to the bottom so the plants wrap around us,
benevolent and terrible?
I'm dressed in gray and although I don't look it
I'm a woman in a ghetto
I'm hundreds of years old
none of you know   you don't suspect it
I live in a strange land in a strange world
and they hound me.

alguna vez. algún tiempo

llegar a mí. una casa vacía
y ni un solo tesoro.
todo desierto en las esquinas.
cargo con mi casa inmueble — desperdicio
el silencio en los túneles
ni siquiera secretos. alguien que haya llegado
a besar el piso las hendiduras
pedir a gritos . . . no la saquen del mar
algo que la conmueva.
pero mi casa es como esos caracoles
muertos sobre la arena enquistados
donde todavía suele el mar remover
algún insecto que asoma y huele pero sin habitar.
o el plancton tembloroso latiendo en mi mano en contra.
aunque tampoco estoy ya ni salgo ni regreso.
nadie ve y mira la estructura muerta
de una casa   el desierto
siempre justo con la orilla
su aparición en el límite.
podría precisarse el vacío? existirá la palabra
que lo ate siquiera al precipicio?
alguien culpable de esa pérdida del ser?
alguna muerte tan destructiva como esta de no creer
que existe lo que oímos
de estar así en la orilla a merced
de un aire inquieto de cierto olor a sal

on some occasion, at some time

arrive at me. an empty house
and not a single treasure.
everything deserted in the corners.
I carry my house, a structure — a waste
silence in the tunnels;
not even secrets. someone who may have arrived
to kiss the floor   the cracks
to beg, crying . . . don't take the house out of the sea
something that could move it to pity.
but my house is like those snails
dead on the sand, covered with cysts,
where the sea still dislodges
insects that wink and sniff at the shell without moving in.
or the trembling plankton, beating against my hand.
though I'm not there anymore, I'm not leaving or
    returning.
no one sees, no one watches the dead structure
of a house   the desert
always precisely on the shoreline
its ghost on the border.
could its emptiness be determined? is there any word
that at least connects it to the precipice?
anyone guilty of that loss of being?
any death as destructive as this one, of not believing
that what we hear exists,
of being on the shore at the mercy
of an anxious air with a certain smell of salt

en las paredes viscosas.
no habrá ni el alma del caracol que se fue
ni del que volverá a humillarse conmigo.
desperdicio. eso son las casas vacías.
no regresa el animal con su pasado.
ese paisaje ya no conmueve al mundo.
una playa desierta y una casa sola.

on the sticky walls.
there won't be even the soul of the snail that left
nor of the one that will return to humble itself with me.
waste. that's what the empty houses are.
the animal with its past doesn't return.
that landscape no longer affects the world.
a deserted beach and an empty house.

la rue de mauvaises herbes

vivo conmigo en un carrusel de mentira que gira y gira para adentro. fumo en la pipa de George Sand, tabaco negro de países lejanos que nunca conoceré. me pinto el pelo de dorado, brillante: cristal de lalic en mis ojos, abajo, la rue de mauvaises herbes. camino, mientras el cristal plástico del sol sigue arriba abovedando Les Halles, comemos una manzana roja de verdad y amanece. soy esta sonámbula que cruza una y otra vez las sensaciones que no tuvo, bajo un pequeño fuego cósmico de hornear pasteles íntimos: para adentro, para adentro, doblándome, existiendo en mí y mintiendo, mirando el desfile y los abanderados que otra vez quieren ser multitud. yo ajena, recibo el polvo de los años 0, escucho los mítines lejanos y saboreo una manzana roja. trato de incorporarme al ruido de los orgasmos intelectuales, pero estoy muerta, muerta y vegetal. bajo mis zapatos prestados, el carrusel de dios donde nunca estuvo. trato de incorporarme y en la fotografía me pinto el vientre: ella se ha ido y se ha ahorcado contra mí muchas veces en un sueño también brillante y repetido. si alguien me trajo, la puso en mí, alguien la llevará. ellos regresan tan mustios tan cansados de cualquier cosa por las calles contrarias, por los cruces. la jarra de lalic quiebra en mis manos. seré feliz? es mejor que regrese y sea yo, definiti–vamente, para mi ocio y soledad conmigo. en Les Halles está amaneciendo y en mi pequeño reloj murciélago de alquiler acariciaré las horas que no estuve nunca aquí, nunca en ninguna parte, siempre ahogada en mis planetas

la rue de mauvaises herbes

I and myself live in a toy carousel that spins, spins inward. I smoke George Sand's pipe, black tobacco from distant countries I'll never see. I dye my hair gold, shining. Lalique crystal in my eyes. below, *la rue de mauvaises herbes*. I walk while the sun's pliant crystal goes on arching over Les Halles, we eat a truly red apple and dawn breaks. I'm this sleepwalker who again and again encounters sensations she never had, under a small cosmic fire for baking intimacies: inward, inward, bending, existing in me and telling lies, watching the parade and the flagbearers who want once again to form a multitude. I, distant, receive the dust of the first decade, I listen to the faraway rallies and savor a red apple. I try to get up and join the noise of the intellectual orgasms, but I'm dead, dead, vegetable. below my borrowed shoes, god's carousel, where he never was. I try to get up, and I paint my womb on the photograph: sleepwalker has gone away, she has defied me many times by hanging herself in a dream, one that glitters and repeats, if someone brought me, if they put her in me, someone will take her away. so withered, so world-weary, they return by the cross-streets, through the intersections. the Lalique jar breaks in my hands. will I be happy? it's better for my inactive and solitary self that I go back and be myself, definitively. in Les Halles dawn is breaking and on my little borrowed watch, flying outside time, I'll fondle the hours when I was never here, never anywhere, always drowning on my watery planets, submerged in that humid intensity.

de agua, sumergida en esa intensidad húmeda. porque nunca me conociste, sólo tuviste la idea de esa mancha que sospecho se proyectó en el muro, o el reflejo por instantes de cristal abovedado sobre nuestras cabezas, sobre figuras que formamos para un recuerdo de paja o de metal: nunca, nunca me conociste. transeúnte de estas calles con mi tabaco oscuro y mi boina de colegial conmemorando algo perdido. no pueden comprender; confrontan. me encontré en esta calle de las malas yerbas, tú entrabas por la puerta principal, yo contraria, con mi espacio de pensar hacía contraseñas para que amaneciera contra la noche de las brujas, de las estúpidas walkirias. tú no eres más que ajeno y mortal: neblina de que tocamos otro ser aparecido, que nos reconciliamos con su pérdida anterior y definitiva. tú también saliste de mi invento, de mi necesidad de sujeción y en mi consuelo, acaricio este vientre, como si fuera mi vientre, un vientre extraño de mujer que copia una manera común de existencia y prepara un mantel mentido de ilusión, pero espera también una vida alternativa y en la cabeza de su cubierta hay un olor inteligente. descuélgala, todavía va a nacer, va a nacer. todavía puede dormir contigo a la intemperie y soñar que es la fiesta, mezclarse con los que aparentan resucitar y se besan y huyen, ella busca tocar ese cristal áspero de lalic, sonarlo muchas veces con los nudillos, vivir sin su apariencia, pero te has levado la jarra y han entrado también los fascistas, los cordeles, las sogas para ahorcar a los semiseres que renuncian a la cordura de la posesión

because you never met me, you only had the idea of a stain, which I suspect projected itself onto the wall, or the moment-by-moment reflection of crystal arching over our heads, over figures we turn into keepsakes of straw or metal: you never, never met me. walking these streets with my dark tobacco and my high-school beret, commemorating something lost. they can't understand; they're confrontational. I found myself on this weed-covered street, you were entering by the main door, I from the opposite side; given room to think, I made up passwords so that day would break against the witches' night, night of the stupid valkyries. you're nothing more than distant and mortal: fog in which we touch another ghostly figure that we reconcile with its prior and definitive loss. you too emerged from my invention, from my need for submission, and as my consolation I fondle this womb, as if it were my womb, the strange womb of a woman who copies a common sort of existence and lays out a tablecloth fabricated from illusion, but who also hopes for an alternative life, and at the head of table there's a whiff of intelligence. cut her down, she's still going to be born, she'll be born. she can still sleep outdoors with you and dream that it's the party, blend in with the ones who seem to come back to life, kiss each other, run away. she tries to tap that harsh Lalique crystal, to sound it out with her knuckles, to live without its appearance, but you've taken the jar away; and the fascists, the cords, the ropes all got in as well to hang the half-beings who renounce the sanity of possession, and now

y ya no queda nada adentro de vida alternativa, de mí conmigo, de carrusel para comenzar a la entrada del tiempo permanente de Les Halles, o en las oscuras aproximaciones a los contactos de las malas yerbas inundadas de voces y voces y mítines que no dicen nada tampoco. por eso está, estoy, sola y perdida en la conmemoración de mi manzana roja, de mi consuelo suficiente en su sabor, conmigo y con ella, con el recuerdo holográfico de ti, de haberte tocado al mirar por el tragaluz sobre las siluetas ennegrecidas de los templos. ¿te llevaré conmigo de este museo hasta la realidad?

nothing remains of the alternative life inside, of me inside myself, of the carousel that begins the entrance into permanent time at Les Halles; nothing remains of the uncertain attempts to experience the intertwining of the weeds, flooded with voices and voices and rallies that don't say anything anymore. that's why she is, I am, alone and lost in the commemoration of my red apple, of my sufficient consolation in its taste, with myself and with the apple, with the holographic memory of you, of having touched you when I looked through the skylight over the darkened silhouettes of the temples. will I take you with me from this museum to reality?

las vigas

en el cuadrado que es una herradura
los encontrábamos cada vez
en ese lugar donde las vigas
son más anchas.
debajo de nosotros hay losas
— dicen que son estables
y que reencarnaremos
sobre esta arquitectura mezclada.
ella anda hoy sólo con un arete en la oreja derecha
y él va cabizbajo.
laboriosamente las manos que hicieron estas cosas
contra posibles derrumbes
no han albergado más que lo efímero.
él va con un arete en la oreja izquierda
y ella va cabizbaja.
observamos las vigas que soportan tanto peso.
mi vida está ladeada
los demás colocan travesaños.
apoyo el centro de la mano contra el muro
y el arco agita
la humedad   el vicio de la herrumbre.
en qué sitio hacemos las paredes los muros
las cosas personales?
en qué lugar quedamos presos de los hábitos
y la tradición sin ser alucinados?
bajamos del ring de las apuestas
de la escenografía de los mundos posibles

the rafters

in the square that is a horseshoe
we found them every time
in that place where the rafters
are wider.
under us are gravestones
— it's said they're stable
and we'll reincarnate ourselves
on this mixed architecture.
all she's wearing today is an earring in her right ear
and he goes along, looking down.
laboriously, the hands that built these things up
against possible collapses
have sheltered only what won't last.
he wears an earring in his left ear
and she goes along, looking down.
we examine the rafters that support so much weight.
my life is tilted
the others put up crossbeams.
I press the center of my hand against the wall
and the arch shakes
humidity   vice of rust.
where do we put partitions   walls
personal things?
where do we remain, prisoners of habit
and tradition, without being taken in?
we get down from the betting ring
from the scenery of possible worlds

de la pasión por las ventanas
mi vida está?
me acuesto sobre el piso caliente del verano
en diciembre dónde estás?
se apuesta a los caballos a la sal a los hombres.
puedo contemplar las vigas que empiezan
a resentirse por el peso de los años
las vigas han de ser reforzadas.
las profundas pasiones. se hacen ligaduras y arden
en el cuadrado del infierno
que es una herradura.

from the passion through the windows
my life is?
I make my bed on summer's hot ground
in December   where are you?
they bet on horses   on salt   on men
I can see rafters starting
to weaken from the weight of the years
the rafters must be reinforced.
profound passions. they bond and burn
in hell's square
that is a horseshoe.

poliedros

ahora puedo dormir y olvidar que estaba esperando, me echo encima la frazada y tomo el jugo que sin querer se derrama sobre el mantel tejido. es una mancha enrojeciendo hasta la cama y mi cuerpo: lo esconderé, porque tras la puerta que da al pasillo se arrastra el ojo, la posesión, la incertidumbre . . . derivar en lo inmóvil sin antes ni después . . . también puedo levantarme y andar por la casa mirando a esos niños que crecieron tan raros y son míos. los miro, los toco: son míos y me vuelvo a echar porque no sé nada del tiempo. desde hace tantos y tantos milenios — no sé cómo contarlos — desde hace tantos milenios estoy inmóvil. pero aún me levanto de la frazada, salgo de allí y me recobro. con la débil-mala luz que hay sobre la máquina de escribir, desnuda, me siento. la huella del líquido se ha derramado en mis uñas: a todo lo que hago le falta centro, algo que yo misma comprenda, que yo sepa saber. le falta literatura — has dicho. no sabes el tamaño real de mi metáfora? ayer traté de explicártelo, un concepto en toda mi vida: no romper la inocencia, aunque para ella tengamos que mentir — mentir no es la palabra —, que matar. tal vez saber querer qué cosa es principio, inicio de la posesión y la incertidumbre, partir de lo que tiene forma y que la des, yo vago hacia atrás, retrotraigo la imagen, la pongo de nuevo sobre la primerísima vez, para conseguirla, para conquistarla. es una corrección aboluta de la metáfora inicial, para perfeccionarla, para que salga

polyhedrons

now I can sleep and forget that I was waiting, I throw the blanket over myself and start drinking my juice, which accidentally spills onto the woven spread. it's a spot reddening out toward the bed and my body: I'll hide it, because behind the door to the hallway, the eye slithers, and so do possession and uncertainty . . . ending up motionless with no before or after . . . I can get up and walk around the house, looking at these children who grew up to be so strange and are mine. I look at them, I touch them: they're mine and I go back to lie down because I know nothing about time. for so many many millennia — I don't know how to count them — for so many millennia I've been motionless. but I still get up off the blanket, I get out of bed and pull myself together. with weak-bad light on the typewriter, nude, I sit down. the liquid's trace has spread under my fingernails: everything I do lacks a center, something I myself may understand, that I might find out how to know. literature is missing — you've said. don't you know the real scope of my metaphor? yesterday I tried to explain it to you, concept shaping my entire life: not to crush innocence, even if we have to lie for it — to "lie" isn't the word — to kill. maybe to know what a beginning is, initiating possession and certainty, starting from the existing form and what you add to it. I wander backwards, retake the image, put it down again on top of the very first time, to get it, to conquer it. it's an absolute correction of the initial metaphor, to perfect it, to make it come out like what I

cómo fue que la vi, que la pensé, para hacerla volviendo. desnuda en la máquina: la máquina del tiempo — simulacro ridículo que sólo anda, al después, en esta otra máquina vacía, ella y yo, buscamos la virginidad, la entrega, el sueño, la locura y algo que fuera a ser yo . . . algo sin asidero, sin una misma sobra de recuerdo que interrumpirá y fijara ese discurso como entre cristales . . . por ejemplo, el paso por la orilla de un río donde uno, alguna vez, podía hundirse y la alegría de esa belleza que tiene el aire golpeándonos y haciéndonos frágiles a punto de caer contra el agua con una cesta de manteles manchados de frutas ácidas en vacaciones. si se perdió ese instante y yo no finjo que lo quiero poseer, cómo era el atardecer que se fue mientras caminábamos y la yerba estaba crecida y de un verde veronés? cómo era? lo recordarás? ahora también puedo dormir y olvidar que estaba esperando. no es importante, estoy sobre las dunas. claro, hace mucho tiempo que estoy loca — como piensas. es la mirada que se vuelve desierto cuando los otros no comienzan conmigo, quieren seguir adelante, saber que saben, lo sé: les humilla un poco, bastante, el olvido de las cosas de aprendieron. pero yo ignoro, yo quiero que lo vuelvan a hacer, que lo descubran acelerándose a la inversa: que no me hagan responsable de todo lo que hice o lo que vi. los niños son raros, han crecido. se acercan, me descubren, me hacen de su imagen, se llaman, buscan a una que no conozco aquí, a una que se ha ido: otro simulacro de pequeños papeles recortados

saw, like what I thought, to make it while returning. nude
inside the typewriter: a time machine, a ridiculous simu–
lacrum who just walks, toward the after, in this other empty
machine, the time machine and I, we look for virginity, we
deliver it, the dream, the insanity and something I was going
to be . . . something without a grip, without an overflow of
memory to interrupt and hold that discourse, as if among
crystallizations . . . for example, the footstep on a riverbank
when you could have fallen in, happiness from the beauty
of the air beating us toward the water, until we almost fell
in with our basket of blankets acid-spotted from summer
fruit. if that instant got lost and I don't pretend I want to
possess it, what was that lost afternoon like while we were
walking and the grass had grown tall and veronese-green?
what was it like? do you remember it? now I can sleep and
forget that I was waiting. it's not important. I'm on top of
the dunes. of course, I've been crazy for a long time — as
you think. it's the gaze that empties out when the others
don't start out with me, they want to keep moving forward,
to know what they know, I know it: it humiliates them a
little, enough, to forget the things they learned. but I don't
notice it, I want them to go back to doing it, for them to
find it accelerating inversely: for them not to make me re-
sponsible for everything I did or saw. the kids are strange,
they've grown. they approach, they find me, they make me
in their image, they call to each other, they look for a
woman unknown to me here, who has gone: another
simulacrum made of small colorful trimmed papers, they

de color, esas astillas me cuelgan de sus brazos, de sus frases. también soy yo la que buscaban, o tú también, perseguidos. todos petrifican algo inconstante para poseerlo, lo que se tiene que llamar amor. ya te lo dije, yo sólo quiero entrar en lo inmóvil sin antes y después, es un ejercicio de atención, te lo repito. no me hago responsable de ningún fragmento, de ninguna sensación verdadera. porque la vida que existe estaba hecha antes, cuando llegué y ahora puedo dormir y olvidar que estaba esperando. al contrario, tú quieres hacerla, que se haga, crees que la estás haciendo para ti, como los otros, esas mentiras: comprenderla. yo llegué y me puse bajo la mancha enrojecida, porque había un poco de frío en mis muslos y habíamos caminado y caminado por entre las yerbas de un verde veronés — aunque todos los días hacíamos lo mismo: recortábamos las cosas que iban a suceder, les dábamos un pequeño espacio-molde para que vivieran, con aquellas tijeras usadas —¡qué espanto!, como si siempre hubiera un después, un elegante final para fabricar las cosas que ocurrieron y no ocurrieron — la metáfora que se pierde en la orilla opuesta del río — y acaso ocurrirán?

hang those pieces on me with their hands, from their sentences. I'm the woman they were looking for, you too, we're all pursued. everyone freezes something inconstant in order to possess it, which has to be called love. I already told you, all I want to find in motionlessness is the before and the after, it's an exercise in attention, I tell you again. I don't take responsibility for any fragment, for any true sensation. because the existing life was made before, when I got here, and now I can sleep and forget that I was waiting. in contrast, you want to do it, you want it done, you think you're making it for yourself, like the others, those lies: to understand it. I arrived and got under the reddened spot, because my thighs were a little cold and we had walked and walked between the veronese-green grasses — although every day we did the same thing: we trimmed out the things that were going to happen, we gave them a small opening where they could live, with those used scissors — scary!, as if there were always an after, an elegant ending to invent the things that happened and that didn't happen — metaphor that gets lost on the river's opposite bank — and maybe those things will happen?

una muchacha loca como los pájaros

una extraña ha venido
a compartir mi cuarto en esta casa . . .
una muchacha loca como los pájaros
— Dylan Thomas

espacio de mi puerta
una muchacha loca entra en mi cuarto
ya no soy yo
le presto esta cabeza
una cabeza oscurecida en el estanque del espejo.
es ella la que llega?
con un cambio de sombrero rozará el ala
su calma   su tristeza.
espacio de mi puerta
entre el laberinto y el voltearme estaba sola
por eso tuve que inventarla
ponerle estos zapatos
hacerla caminar sobre mí.
una imagen de la que uno nace es la única manera
de nacer dos veces.
alguien vendrá después y la apartará?
saltará del fondo donde se esconde la que vuelve
a sobrevivir
la que ha llegado y no sabe dónde está?
la muchacha que empezó adentro
ha terminado el tiempo de su fin:

a girl mad as birds

*a stranger has come
to share my room in this house . . .
a girl mad as birds . . .*
— Dylan Thomas

space of my door
a mad girl enters my room
now I'm not me
I lend her this head
a head tarnished in the mirror's pondwater.
with a change of hats her calm   her sadness
will scrape against the frame.
space of my door
between the labyrinth and the changing of my mind, I
    was alone.
that's why I had to invent her
put these shoes on her
make her walk over me.
the only way to be born twice
is for an image to give birth.
will someone come along later and take her away?
will she jump out of the background, where she's hiding,
    the one who continues
to survive?
the one who has arrived and doesn't know where she is?
the girl who began inside
has lived out her purpose:

esa cámara oscura   ese instante en que detrás del lente
o entre ese lente y yo
estaba su ojo jamás la realidad ni la certeza
por eso tuve que inventarla
sin saber   sin querer.
espacio de mi puerta
tengo los dedos ásperos de tanto andar contra el agua
apoyando lo que quema y arde
vendrá por fin? modelaré este invento
para sentar otra vez frente a mis pájaros
a otra muchacha loca en el espejo.
dejémosla fingir
se mueve   me convence
déjenla correr y muerta su sombra contra el río
que ella crea que aparece y se va
me llevará hasta el fin?
se ha quedado dormida sobre el rodillo y su fábula
es así. me toparé en el sitio encontrado
con el vestido que dejó vacío
y la devolveré
sin mí   sin la que fui.
espacio de mi puerta
laberinto prestado. yo casco nueces con los pies.
devuélvela señor y que aparezca
esa misma que quise cuando yo me inventaba.

that *camera obscura* behind the lens in that instant
or between that lens and me
was her eye   never reality or certainty
that's why I had to invent her
unknowingly unintentionally.
space of my door
my toes calloused from walking so long against the
     water's flow
supporting a body that scorches and is consumed
will she arrive at last? I will shape this creation,
I'll sit down again facing my birds
facing another mad girl in the mirror.
we should allow her to pretend
that she moves   she convinces me
let her run, her shadow already expired on the river
she creates, it appears and disappears
will she take me to the river's end?
she has fallen asleep on my rolling pin and that's her
story. I'll bump into myself in the space
found inside the dress she left empty
and I'll return her
without me   without the woman I was.
space of my door
loaned labyrinth. I crack nuts with my feet.
give her back, so maybe she'll appear
the same woman I intended when I invented myself.

Violet Island

. . . yo conocí a cierto hombre, un hombre extraño.
cuidaba cada día y cada noche la luz de su faro,
un faro en la medianía que no indicaba mucho,
un faro pequeño para embarcaciones de poco nivel
y oscuros pueblos de pescadores. allí, en su isla,
él intercambiaba con su faro las sensaciones
esperando cada día, cada noche esa otra luz
que no vigila la persecución de algún objeto,
esa otra luz que no ilumina nada,
otra luz reflexiva, que cruza hacia adentro,
la distancia entre el puerto seguro del sitio
y el ojo que mira volver, por encima y transparente,
la ilusión provisional que se eterniza:
esa curva del ser tendido junto al faro
sin precaución ni límite, para ser o tener
lo que imperfectamente somos, nada más,
que soñar lo que sueñe y estar donde está
sobre las quietas aguas y apagarlo todo en el cuadro
de un día y ser nuevo otra vez hacia la madrugada
junto al faro pequeño y perdido de Aspinwoll
sin siquiera imaginar que existe algún deseo
fuera de desear la breve luz que cae, anocheciendo,
sobre las quietas aguas y los sonidos muertos ya

Violet Island

. . . I met a certain man, a strange man.
every day and every night he tended the lamp in his
    lighthouse,
a run-of-the-mill lighthouse that didn't mark much of
    anything,
a small lighthouse for ships of little importance
and obscure fishermen's villages. there, on his island,
he exchanged sensations with his lighthouse,
waiting every day, every night for another light
that doesn't watch over the persecution of anything,
another light that illuminates nothing,
another reflective light, moving inward,
crossing the distance between the safe port
and the eye, overhead and transparent, that watches the
    return
of temporary illusion   that becomes eternal:
curve of that self stretched out next to the lighthouse
without precaution or limit, to be or to have
what we imperfectly are, nothing more,
to dream what he may and to be where he is
above the quiet waters and to shut off everything in one
    day's
expanse, to be new again at daybreak
next to the small, lost lighthouse of Aspinwoll
without even imagining that any desire could exist
other than desire for the brief light that falls, darkening,
onto quiet waters, deadened sounds

de aquellas olas, que en otro tiempo, fueron su pasión;
su dolor, de gozar y sufrir, un refugio sincero.
como el guardafaros de Aspinwoll, sólo en su faro,
yo me quedé dormida, a pesar de la intensa luz que cae
y sobresale por encima del tiempo, a pesar de la lluvia
golpeando el espejo de los peces blancos,
a pesar de aquella luz espiritual que era su alma,
yo me quedé dormida entre el puerto y la luz,
sin comprender: quería, sólo quería un tiempo más
para volver aprendiendo, no sobre la resaca de la
    conmiseración
donde atan su mástil los desesperados;
no la fortuna auténtica de vivir sin saber, sin darse
    cuenta;
no la luz provisional que se eterniza y finge lo que
    seremos
o el miedo de poseer la realidad opaca, intrascendente.
yo quería la vida sólo por el placer de morir, sobre las
    quietas aguas,
junto a los peces blancos y estaba impaciente
porque sucediera todavía la reedición de mi inconsciente
para que alguien hallara allí lo no tocado, la otra voz,
no de este ser intermediario, un cuerpo para medir las
    grietas
bajas; un cuerpo para la violación de un yo
    impracticable:

of those waves, which once were his passion;
his pain, a real refuge from happiness and suffering.
like the lighthouse-keeper of Aspinwoll, alone in his
    lighthouse,
I fell asleep, in spite of intense light that falls
and stands out beyond time, in spite of rain,
beating against a whitefish mirror,
in spite of that spiritual light that was his soul,
I fell asleep between the port and the light,
without understanding: I wanted, I just wanted some
    more time
to learn, not about the undertow of commiseration
where the desperate ones set their mast;
not the authentic fortune of living without knowledge,
    without realization;
or the temporary light that turns eternal and gives a false
    illusion of what we are,
or the fear of possessing opaque and unimportant reality.
I wanted life only for the pleasure of dying on the quiet
    waters
next to the whitefish and I was impatient
because the reprinting of my unconscious would still be
    going on
so someone could find what hadn't been touched there,
    the other voice,
not the voice of this intermediary being, a body to
    measure against little
crevices; a body for the violation of an impracticable I:

yo me quedé dormida, inconsecuente, en la imaginación
de ese otro en la distancia, suficientemente avanzada
para tener iluminación propia en Aspinwoll, pero
    fracasada
también oscurecida, como el guardafaros sobre las
    quietas aguas
de lo que imperfectamente somos, en la medianía
de un faro que no indicaba mucho, a través de la lluvia
    cálida
y real de lo imposible.

soy Fela. no te conozco. este cuerpo con que vendré no
    es mío
la aparición será otra cosa: como despeñarse, una
    avería,
un silencio.
y si pierdo? o si gano? o si atravieso el foso vertical?

me acerco a los animales como únicos sobrevivientes
maravillados con el ocio de la luz
y estos pastos vacíos que atravieso con horror
y llamándolos. me acerco a dónde van, a dónde van
    todos?
buscando dónde asir lo que hubo de cierto
y sin espejismos del desastre del ser como únicos
    sobrevivientes
del faro en su vértigo tal vez los haga comprender mi
    intención

I fell asleep, inconsequential, in the imagination
of that other person in the distance, sufficiently
    advanced
to have my own enlightenment at Aspinwoll, but failed
and obscured   like the lighthouse-keeper above the quiet
    waters
of what we imperfectly are, by the run-of-the-mill
lighthouse that didn't mark much of anything, through
    the warm and real
rain of impossibility.

I'm Fela. I don't know you. this body with which I'll come
    isn't mine —
the apparition will be something else: like falling off a
    cliff, a breakdown,
a silence.
and if I lose? or if I win? or if I cross over the abyss?

I approach animals as if they were sole survivors,
astonished at the light's idleness
and these empty fields that I cross in horror,
calling to them.   I approach   where are they going,
    where are they all going?
looking for a place to grasp something definite from the
    past,
without disastrous illusions of being sole survivors
from that vertiginous lighthouse; maybe they can
    understand my intention

de contar todavía alguna sombra, alguna luz.
no quiero domesticar a nadie más.
que ellos penetren con su sabiduría en mis voces
y se acerquen sin ser, sin pedir, sin darse cuenta
pero conociendo desde el doblado ojo enrojecido, otro
   lenguaje,
otra profundidad que no marque lo seguro, ningún
   término,
ninguna valentía. sólo estar donde estamos y posarnos
como inteligencias diferentes en la sensación,
   prestándonos
dolor, angustia, alguna llama estable.

y ahora dime . . . gime al oído
fue una ciudad con puerto.
los nombres de sus barcos profundos
anclaron alguna vez aquí.
nombres raros con esmaltes muy fuertes
y encendidos.
estábamos rodeados de horizonte y de agua,
porque los puertos permiten olvidar y recibir,
olvidar y volver.
fue una ciudad con puerto
donde ya no se ha ido ni ha vuelto nadie más.
una niebla permanente cubre la tela de fondo
todavía azul y humedecida del invierno
y el descolorido ondear de las banderas
agujereadas por la sombra.

to still tell the story of some shadow, some light.
I don't want to tame anyone else.
let them penetrate my voices with their wisdom
and approach without being, without requesting, without
   realizing,
but through the doubled, reddened eye, knowing another
   language,
another profundity that won't locate security, or any
   limit,
or any bravery. only being where we are and settling
as different intelligences into sensation, allowing us
pain, anguish, some stable flame.

and now tell me . . . moan in my ear
it was a city with a port.
the names of its deep ships
once anchored here.
odd names with strong,
shining varnishes.
we were surrounded by horizons and by water,
because ports allow forgetting and receiving,
forgetting and returning.
once it was a city with a port
where now no one else has come or gone.
a permanent fog covers the backdrop,
still blue and dampened by the winter,
and the discolored waving of the flags,
riddled with holes by the shadow.

si bien antes fue un límite
cuando salías a mirarlo y correr
ahora es sólo la apariencia de un límite
el sonido de las sirenas muertas
que ya no suenan a través de ti
ni se confunden ni te llaman.
pero en dónde está el puerto?
¿y los barcos?
¿y el faro?
¿y los hombros de los marineros convidándote
a otros puertos oscuros?

if a long time ago it was a boundary
when you went out to look at it and run
now it's just the appearance of a boundary
the call of dead sirens
who no longer sound through you
or get confused or speak to you.
but where is the port?
and the ships?
and the lighthouse?
and the shoulders of the sailors inviting you
to other dark ports?

ídolo del crepúsculo

mi deseo en la huella de mi miedo . . . mi deseo es la huella de mi miedo. frente al espejo, un rostro serio de mujer madura me observa (escasez de los vellos del pubis, antes muy negros). muslos unidos, separados; unidos, separados, senos con bolas oscuras en las puntas (separados) como los de tía Adelfa. mi mano sobre mí. nalgas bajas, demasiado tristes, fláccidas? una divinidad acecha tras mi oreja y algo que no se presenta, no se ve, me adentra en la especie, pareja de mí, qué más puedo ofrecer? mi pie perfecto que no ha envejecido, dulcísimo. me acerco y me separo raramente. me gusta mi lirismo porque engendra en el cuerpo un yo (otro) que detrás del cristal, lentamente, se hunde sobre la cama y abro las ventanas para que entre con el resplandor, la única nube baja del día. me desnudo, me desnudo y no hay mí. abro y cierro las piernas (expansión y contracción del universo) se difumina alrededor, me integro y no hago nada. cualquier gesto sería todopoderoso frente a mi espera. lubricada, frente al espejo, acabo de conocer mi cuerpo y de rechazarlo porque él a veces pretende poseer un espacio, una oblicuidad que me distrae de lo continuo, de la interrupción del paisaje (intimidad contenida en un pequeño pote y azucenas). soy más que él. mi delgadez, su arritmia, la oblación. fin de semana, pequeño y sin ceremonias, cómo subvertir el lado oscuro del ser contra esos límites? me niego a representarme otra vez en esas líneas o silencios que culminan en amarillo tras una forma y su vaciedad (mancha

twilight's idol

my desire in the imprint of my fear . . . my desire is the imprint of my fear. in front of the mirror, a mature woman's serious face observes me (scarcity of soft pubic hair, once very black). thighs together, apart; together, apart, breasts (apart) with dark balls on the nipples like Aunt Adelfa's. my hand upon me. sagging buttocks, pathetic, flabby? a deity lurks behind my ear and something that doesn't come forward, isn't seen, moves me into the species, my mate, what more can I offer? my perfect foot which has not aged, so soft. I come together and separate strangely. I like my lyricism because it generates an I (an other) in my body who sinks down on the bed behind the glass, slowly, and I open the windows so that the day's only low cloud enters with the glare. I undress, I undress and there's no me. I open and close my legs (expansion and contraction of the universe), it disappears around me, I pull myself together and I do nothing. any gesture would be all-powerful in the face of my expectations. lubricated, across from the mirror, I've just discovered my body and rejected it because sometimes it tries to possess a space, an obliqueness that distracts me from what is continuous, from the interruption of the landscape (intimacy contained in a small flowerpot with lilies). I am more than my body. my slenderness, its arrhythmia, oblation. the weekend, small and without ceremonies, how does one subvert the dark side of the self against those limits? I refuse to imagine myself again in those lines or silences culminating in yellow behind a shape

oscura bajo la nalga derecha). pobre cráter. mi ser no es esto. algo más comprometedor que la aceptación o el rechazo; algo más bajo y tibio que una superficie (orgullo de poseerme en mí y no en otro que me obtiene doblemente). ha empezado esta guerra: la flaccidez cuando germina es mental. te gusta mi flaccidez? es lúcida. te obsesiona mi pobretud y el excremento verde sobre el fondo de la taza rosada? eres tú, un cuerpo ancho para romper mi intimidad, pero no soy dos: no vivir, no vivir entraña la vida (la vida que se vive perece y escapa) no amar, no amar entraña el amor . . . no pensar, no pensar, entraña un pensamiento. ella con su bata raída en los codos, en las tardes se frotaba el pubis con pedazos de hielo seco, se frotaba y se frotaba frente a la ventana, entre el resplandor y la única nube baja del día. él la veía. una virginidad para el hielo boreal (labios abiertos por el frío quemante del hielo muerto) después, se despertaba contra el pequeño seto con el dolor de sus imágenes. la nube había desaparecido. era entonces una falsa nube nacida de su contacto con el hielo, un desafío al paisaje. cada tarde un suicidio y el olvido de la caída anterior (porque un suicidio debe ser obsesivo en sí mismo) salto orgásmico, orgón. corre y tómala, esa también soy yo (figura de mi madre saliendo de la bañera antigua con sus ojos verdes atrapados en un pubis de niña) qué horror no ser ya ella. tú me pides que sea indiscreta y te cuente cosas al oído. yo me acerco muchísimo, pero en vano. no tengo palabras, ni canciones, ni otras escenas frente a este árbol

and its emptiness (dark stain under the right buttock). poor
crater. my self is not this. something more committed than
acceptance or rejection; something lower and warmer than
a surface (proud of controlling myself inside one self and
not in another that splits me into two). this war has begun:
when the flabbiness sprouts, it's mental. do you like my
flabbiness? it is clear. are you obsessed with my poverty
and the green excrement on the bottom of the pink cup?
it's you, a broad body to break my intimacy, but I am not
two: not living, not living involves life (life that is lived per-
ishes and escapes) not loving, not loving involves love . . .
not thinking, not thinking involves thought. she, with her
robe threadbare at the elbows, in the afternoon she would
rub her pubis with pieces of dry ice, she would rub and rub
herself in front of the window, between the glare and the
day's only low cloud. he would see her, a virginity for the
northern ice (open lips for the burning cold of the dead
ice). afterwards, she would wake up against the small hedge
with the pain of her images. the cloud had disappeared. it
would be, then, a false cloud born of her contact with the
ice, a challenge to the landscape. each afternoon a suicide
and the lost memory of the previous fall (because a suicide
should be obsessive within itself), orgasmic leap, orgon.
run and take her, she too is me (the figure of my mother
getting out of the old bathtub with her green eyes fixed on
a girl's pubis), how awful not to be her anymore. you ask
me to be indiscreet and whisper things in your ear. I get
very close, but in vain. I don't have words, or songs, or

frondoso y el aroma de esas yerbas espinosas que se enredan en los dedos, por hacer algo. nada que me acepte. mi trampa abierta en su perfecta transparencia y vacía soy yo. con los dientes metálicos bajo el agua de vaso resistiendo una ancianidad que sobrepasa mi conciencia, o una tajada en el tiempo — abierta, todavía cortante — que me haga descender empujándome a ser otra vez ídolo del crepúsculo. no habrá más forma, cuerpo doblegado en sus curvas, inarmonías, sinuosidades: olores transitorios que se han quedado cuando abro la ventana y las piernas y pido perdón sobre el fango, sólo sangre, estiércol y sangre coagulándose (paciencia y mansedumbre que resbala en cualquier lodo) y la comisura me sonríe obedeciendo a una extraña pureza de mirarme — el ser ya alguna otra — inconforme también de su eterno retorno (el objeto de la fantasía es también huidozo). Narciso, o el amor del hombre como amor imposible (la jugada del espirítú consistirá en el hacer de los objetos una creación del sujeto, en tomar la realidad por una fantasma creado por el autor). obsesión de descubrirla cayendo sobre el seto oscuro — nadie me había prevenido — ser simplemente una historia que se va repitiendo, consumiendo, lentamente contra el rompenubes.

other scenes opposite that leafy tree and the scent of those spiny weeds; they get tangled up in your fingers, just to be doing something. nothing that accepts me. I am my open, empty trap in its perfect transparency. with the metallic teeth underwater in the glass resisting an old age that overcomes my conscience, or a slice in time — open, still cutting — that makes me go down, pushing me to be, again, twilight's idol. there will be no more form, no body yielding in its curves, discordances, sinuousities: transitory odors that remain when I open the window and my legs and I ask forgiveness in the mud, just blood, dung curdling with blood (patience and meekness that slip on any mud), and the corner of the mouth smiles at me, obeying a strange purity by looking at me — the self already some other — not accepting her eternal return either (the object of the fantasy is evasive too). Narcissus, or man's love as impossible love (the play of the spirit will consist of turning objects into the creation of the subject, of taking reality as a ghost created by the author). the obsession with discovering her while she's falling over the dark hedge — nobody had warned me — to be simply a story that goes on repeating itself, consuming itself, slowly against the cloudbreaker.

luz acuosa

por la ventana de barco, luego de traspasar la tela, envejecida y floreada de una pequeña cortina blanca, entraba una luz acuosa que me hacía mirar — aún sin querer — las rajaduras del edificio, el peso de los tanques de agua destapados, las vigas de hierro que han perdido su revestimiento y crujen al pasar las bandadas de palomas que bajan, suben, se esconden de este resplandor de marzo, huyen quizá. la niña duerme con fiebre y él, en el piso (proa) sobre una colchoneta. los gatos buscan también alguna humedad y se dispersan sobre el cemento — ahora gris, después rojo — y yo pienso, más bien saboreo entre la luz — repito — acuosa y esa lana que protege los restos de guatas de un colchón agotado por el peso también, su lengua fina entrando en mi boca. la punta más afilada de esa lengua que me causó cierto rechazo entonces, y ahora vuelvo a saborear (con algo de la humedad de un verano que bajará sin tregua a calentarnos) y las palomas se desplazan otra vez equidistantes. él ya se fue. y apetece una lluvia finísima contra la piel que hierve, que late (yo me levanto a escribir para vencer ese horror por las distancias, ese temblor por las pérdidas) la nube se ha hecho una masa gris que se aproxima y calienta (un cerebro) para tapar cualquier visibilidad por la ventana barco anclado de mi cuarto. tendré que mover la punta fina de la pluma otra vez por su lengua. no puedo comprender que un cuerpo grande así, termine en esa prolongación de estilete. me desagrada la debilidad, ahora

watery light

through the porthole, then passing through the old and flowered cloth of a small white curtain, a watery light entered that made me look — though unwilling — at the cracks in the building, the weight of the uncovered water tanks, the iron beams that have lost their casings and creak when the flocks of doves pass, dive, rise, hide from this March splendor, flee perhaps. the girl sleeps with a fever, and he is on the floor (prow) on a cushion. the cats are looking for some moisture as well and they scatter across the cement — now gray, then red — and I think, or rather I taste, between the light — I repeat — the watery light and that wool protecting the remaining stuffing of a cushion also crushed under the weight, his slender tongue entering my mouth. the sharpest point of the tongue that provoked a certain rejection from me then, and now I taste again (with some of the moisture of an oppressive summer heat that will descend mercilessly upon us) and the doves spread out equidistantly again. he has already gone. and there's a craving for a misty rain against the boiling skin, the beating skin (I get up and write to conquer that fear of distances, that trembling over losses) the cloud has become a gray mass (a brain) that approaches and warms in order to obscure any visibility through the anchored ship's window of my room. I'll have to move the pen's fine point over his tongue again. I can't understand how a large body like that can end in its stiletto prolongation. weak-

me gusta. me gusta y duele. masa gris que se aproxima acuosa y vence a mi garganta quemándome (aquella mañana no me atreví, pero que bien se está ahorcajada sobre el pecho, el vientre, la cintura de otro, así: de pie). mi ciudad es una masa caliente con exceso de tejido (sobreabundancia de ser), mucosa prieta, útero que se ensancha y dilapida y llueve algunas veces agua, otras sangre. el ruido de mi ciudad es interior y gris, se ensancha — determinado por las hormonas — que colorean estos suburbios, las azoteas, los entrepisos arenosos o metálicos del sentir (radicalmente ha cambiado la temperatura y un viento helado y fuerte hace mecer las bisagras). hemos comido remolacha hirviendo. aquí y allá, suben amorfos los pedazos de zinc, los veo volar, me sobrecogen. la casa, un barco en medio de las entrañas (varado), hiperplasia de endometrio — ha dicho. habrá mucha sangre, profundas marejadas. o uso los rellenos de algunos animales de Elis, o muñecas de trapo, también lana. todo sirve aquí para aumentar — si es posible esa distinción de cantidad — la angustia. siempre mis amigos se fueron, primero unos, alrededor de los 20, después otros, a través de los 40. años cavando de la vagina hacia el corazón. se aproxima aún más la nube gris. tanta ansiedad por construir una amistad y después, parten (repitiré, volverán, seguro, vuelven profanados para convivir). mientras más me acerco, voy sintiendo los días como páginas (lugar común) y el cuerpo de la obra apurándose por consumir su tiempo blanco. a medida que paso las páginas, convoco algún tono, cierto

ness bothers me, now it pleases me. it pleases me and it pains me. gray mass that is almost watery and conquers my throat, burning me (that morning I didn't dare, but how good it feels, straddling my chest, my belly, another's waist, like that: upright). my city is a hot mass with too much texture (overabundance of being), dark mucus, uterus that expands and wastes away and sometimes rains water, sometimes blood. my city's noise is interior and gray, it expands — determined by hormones — that color these suburbs, the rooftops, the mezzanines, sandy or metallic to the touch (the temperature has changed radically and a strong, cold wind shakes the hinges). we've eaten boiling sugar beet. here and there, pieces of zinc rise amorphously, I see them flying, they overtake me. the house, a ship among the entrails (stranded), hyperplasia of the endometrium — he said. there will be a lot of blood, deep swells. I use the stuffing from some of Elís' animals, or rag dolls, wool too. everything helps here to increase — if the quantifiable distinction is possible — the anguish. my friends were always leaving, first some around age twenty, then others through the forties. years tunneling from my vagina to my heart. the gray cloud draws even closer. so much anxiety over building a friendship and then, they leave (I'll repeat, they will return, surely, they'll return, desecrated, to live together). the closer I get, the more I'm feeling the days as pages (common place) and the body of the work hurrying to consume its white time. as I turn the pages, I summon a certain shade, a certain color, to seem somewhat differ-

color, para que parezca algo diferente. un azul francés, otro azul ultramar, algún áureo. (los ojos que me gustan son color azul acero) aunque acepto las variantes. los días, repito, más allá de un tono (truco), un movimiento oblicuo del color, o la detención por instantes de una nube, como hoy, son idénticos (la sensación de la página que se llena con signos del hastío para detener la muerte, o cambiar). y este ruido que conozco como un malestar, un zumbido que pía la oreja manchándose por una mala prenda (no es oro todavía, siempre es mal vidrio). escribo aquellas páginas que me dan los días con sus diferentes crepúsculos contemplados desde la hamaca (ahí mi lujo, mi obsesión) de preferir mirar la extensión que hace distinto un fin. estaba tan distraida, tan entretenida, que nunca aceptaba la realidad . . . (mi lujo) a la hora del mediodía, con el intenso calor del verano, abrir las piernas y dejar que esa lengua delgada ande otra vez hurgando allí una vía de entrar a la ciudad, de conocer su ruido, saber si yo era cierta a través de una capa de olores puros, o ácidos, mezclados (olores que sobrepasan cualquier ph, tierra, virilidad, femenidad, olores que un perfumista esencial decidió combinar con tonos de rojos, fresa, claro, púrpura) y yo pensando qué estaría descubriendo allí bajo el vértigo, qué fórmula se haría de verdad de su saliva conmigo. una página pasa en el acto de abrir y cerrar las piernas y yo no sé qué estoy haciendo. cuántos sabores iguales, únicos y distintos que tienes que reabsorber para elegir. pero la ciudad, que ha ensanchado sus paredes rajadas (morfología

ent. a French blue, another ultramarine, some gold. (the
eyes I like are steel blue) although I accept variations. the
days, I repeat, beyond a shade (a trick), an oblique move-
ment of color, or a cloud's gradual halting, like today, are
identical (the feeling of the page that fills itself with signs
of weariness to delay death, or to change). and this noise
that I know as discomfort, a buzzing in my ear that reveals
itself as cheap jewelry (it's not gold yet, just plastic). I write
those pages that the days give me with their different twi-
lights contemplated from the hammock (there my luxury,
my obsession) of preferring to watch the expanse that
makes an end distinct. I was so distracted, so entertained,
that I never accepted reality . . . (my luxury) at noon, with
the summer's intense heat, to open my legs and let that
slim tongue wander there again, delving for a way to get
into the city, to meet its noise, to know whether I were true
behind a cape of pure scents, or acid ones, mixed (scents
that exceed any pH, earth, virility, femininity, scents that a
perfume designer decided to combine with shades of red,
strawberry, clear, purple) and I'm wondering what he's dis-
covering there below the vertigo, what formula he's really
making with me out of his saliva. a page turns in the act of
opening and closing my legs and I don't know what I'm
doing. how many identical, unique and different tastes you
have to reabsorb in order to choose. but the city, which
has expanded its cracked walls (morphology of the cell)

de la célula) no se deja penetrar fácilmente. me subo el jean. la vecina gritaba porque vio un paracaídas con su paracaidista caer desde el fondo azulado, josto sobre su azotea — un mercenario, gritó —, y era sólo un aeróstato desviado por el viento (cuando te abrazo hay una reconciliación muy humana del mal, totalmente cálida, cuya emanación — diría — da cuerpo a una presencia in-dispensable para estar así, tan salvados en el miedo). mi barco sigue anclado de esta manera de imaginarse: sucede un día tras otro y todos juntos parten a cambiar su libro vivido, un libro que se cierra por otro nuevo, liso, sin marcas, aún no ajado que enciende un deseo más poderoso que el anterior. (yo soy como un libro con exceso de marcas, subrayados, algunos con plumón azafrán). necesidad de describir la voz del útero: una voz blanda, matinal, grave, que te adormece por ser atendida, muellemente amada dentro de sí, drenando. nadie te acaricia por dentro. tu mamá va a hacer un dulce exquisito, una cosa especial. la remolacha de hoy ya está hirviendo. al fin, somos mujeres. cuando convido, los que convido no están allí. los otros son los que vienen. (Clarise con su vestido verde cosiendo un doblez tras otro que le permite recordar a cada puntada, a cada paso, un poco del pasado) "el Cordero que fue degollado desde la fundación del mundo . . ." Plantagenet con sus ladrillos refractarios empalizando su obsesión; o Stephen Dedalus convertido en el nombre de un gato arrabalero, mis personajes también se fueron. y Virginia y Dinesen y los demás? todos

doesn't allow itself to be penetrated easily. I pull up my jeans. the neighbor lady was shouting because she saw a parachute with its parachutist fall out of the bluish backdrop, right over her rooftop — a mercenary, she shouted — and it was only a hot air balloon blown off course (when I embrace you there is a warm, very human reconciliation to trouble; its emanation — I would say — gives form to a presence that's necessary for being saved through fear). my ship stays at anchor by imagining itself this way: one day follows another and all together they leave to alter their living book, a book that closes for another new one, fresh, without marks, not yet faded, that sparks a desire stronger than the previous one. (I'm like a book with too many marks, underlines, some with a yellow highlighter.) the need to describe the voice of the uterus: a soft, serious voice at dawn that lulls you to sleep when heeded, softly loved within, draining. no one caresses you on the inside. your mama's going to make a delicious treat, something special. today's sugar beet is already boiling. in the end, we are women. when I issue an invitation, those I invite aren't there. the others are the ones who come. (Clarise with her green dress sewing one fold after another letting her recall every stitch, every step, a little of the past) "the Lamb slaughtered since the beginning of the world . . ." Plantagenet with his refractory bricks fortifying his obsession; or Stephen Dedalus changed into the name of an alley cat, my characters left too. and Virginia and Dinesen

71

muertos, muertos o prófugos. paren este juego infernal!
Ricardo Reich sigue riéndose desde el espejo, a la sombra
de un ahorca donde encuentro a Nerval, o el cristalito roto
de la ventana donde, cuando abría las piernas — y los ojos
— veía a Santa Teresa, mirándome. es dulce de remolacha.
esta ciudad que hemos construido lentamente con mate-
ria divina, con muertos y sustancia de útero (angustia por
sobrepasar un estado de angustia (ego) y un pene
tremendo, ya para mí, sólo es literatura). claro, la vecina
que vio al mercenario caer no pensará lo mismo, ahí está
la diferencia, ella espera verdades. un pene es rosado? es
sangre, resina de dragón? es sepia? tal vez siena tostada
(este libro del color me ha hecho comprender que a penas
diviso los matices, sus dolores). a veces me entretengo
recordándolos, los acaricio, recordándolos. tú decías mi
nombre otra vez, como un lamento, como un fin . . . y
entonces, tu cara quedó atrapada allí para siempre, en la
ventana barco, junto a la cortina — que antes fue una saya
blanca — mi bandera de paz. tragué ese semen con miedo
a envenenarme (no era distinto) pero igual, era único. te
poseías en mí. la oreja manchándose con lata color de
desierto. hay aquí un misterio muy singular, qué
degradación debí sufrir a cambio? acaba de pasar la
tempestad y al fondo de los edificios mojados, leve ilusión
de armonía, éxtasis (intensificación o reducción de la
intensidad; los colore fríos y cálidos yuxtapuestos se
intensifican mutuamente). lo perfecto es el cuerpo y la
sangre en los altares.

and the rest? all dead, dead or fugitives. stop this infernal game! Richard Reich keeps laughing from the mirror, at the shadow of a gallows where I find Nerval, or the little broken windowpane where, when I was opening my legs — and my eyes — I could see Saint Teresa, watching me. it's sugar beet spread. this city that we've built slowly with divine matter, with the dead and with uterine substance (anguish about overcoming a state of anguish (ego) and a tremendous penis, now for me, it's just literature). of course, the neighbor lady who saw the mercenary fall won't think the same way, there's the difference, she expects truths. a penis is pink? it's blood, dragon's resin? sepia? maybe burnt sienna (this coloring book has made me understand that it's hard for me to distinguish shades, their pains). sometimes I entertain myself remembering them, I stroke them, remembering them. you were saying my name again, like a lament, like an ending . . . and then, your face stayed trapped there forever, in the ship's window, next to the curtain — which used to be a white skirt — my white flag. I swallowed that semen afraid of poisoning myself (it wasn't any different) but all the same, it was unique. you were possessing yourself in me. your ear reddening with desert-colored paint. here there's quite a singular mystery, what degradation did I suffer in exchange? the storm has just passed and at the foot of the wet buildings, a light illusion of harmony, ecstasy (intensification or reduction of intensity; the cool and warm colors, juxtaposed, intensify each other mutually). perfection is the body and the blood on the altars.

como las cosas caras

. . . sabes cómo es eso? . . . *como las cosas caras, como los días en que ser fiero era dejarse beber* . . . uno sueña, primero con ser, creer que se es, eso que se edificó por dentro, el juego-dibujo que la percepción nos hizo elegir y realizar (ese proyecto sin apenas verificar por qué la elección, con qué conciencia triunfamos contra otras posibles opciones); por qué ésta, casi definitiva, que se llamó nuestra vida y ya siempre es pasado, reconstruido y vuelto a empezar. un eje, una figura que empezamos a conocer desde afuera . . . no te preocupes de la trampa — dijo una voz — la trampa, nada es . . .

estoy debilitándome vertiginosamente, cómo decirte la necesidad, si la necesidad quema, mancha, hace un tizne verdoso sobre las ilusiones; la necesidad está tan cerca que es un atropello, no nos permite un espacio para recorrer la llanura, toda su extensión vastísima y acercarnos y alejarnos otra vez. la necesidad es esa llama que te di, sin ilusión, gastándose, recalentada, la mitad de un sentido . . . *el lujo de ser sólo ahora*, y después? por eso puede ser poder . . .

(. . . hiperrealismo es la necesidad que no le permite un campo a la seducción, es una boca oscura, tragándote y tú quieres esperar alejarte para dar una respuesta, o no darla, tú quieres ver (la boca de Lena, la boca de Katasia, la marca de la boca de otro, la huella) . . . pero la necesidad te

like things that are expensive

. . . you know what that's like? . . . *like things that are expensive, like the days when being fierce meant letting yourself be imbibed* . . . you dream, first about being, about believing that you are, the structure that you built inside, the game-sketch that perception caused us to choose and carry out (that project done almost without verifying why we make the choice, with what conscience we triumph over other possible options); why choose this one, almost definitive, that was called our life and now it's always past, reconstructed, restarted. an axis, a figure we begin to recognize from the outside . . . don't worry about the trap — said a voice — the trap, it's nothing . . .

I'm weakening vertiginously, how can I explain the need to you, if the need burns, stains, leaves a greenish soot on illusions; the need is so close that it runs us over, it leaves us no space to travel around the plains, across all of their vast expanse, to approach each other and to separate again. the need is the flame that I gave you, one with no illusion, expending itself, too hot, half of a meaning . . . *the luxury of existing only now*, and later? that's why it can be power . . .

(. . . hyperrealism is the need that leaves no ground for seduction, it's a dark mouth, swallowing you and you want to wait to pull away until you can give a response, or not give it, you want to see (Lena's mouth, Katasia's mouth, the mark of someone else's mouth, the trace) . . . but the

crucifica en el umbral de toda perspectiva y su crucifixión, no te hará renacer en el campo de cenizas donde quedó, atrás, la esperanza . . .)

. . . una lámpara recalentada, oscura, recorta la sombra de mi mano en el papel. tijeras. busco explicarme la imposible dualidad símbolo-objeto: lo que parece que somos y nos creemos y la realidad. inscribir la memoria de un tiempo en la historia, ser protagónico (agónico) de ese momento, más allá de su representación (sin las parodias de mí misma en el oficio de "lo poético") cómo venir desde allá, escaleras de Leningrado bajando desde la Ajmátova y la nieve hasta mí? . . . estoy enferma de un sueño incurable, de palabras que no se cumplen; de creaciones que crecen con fuerza, pero sin espacio y se desaniman, cuando se estratifican y no se satisfacen. hasta mí llega el orgullo y la enfermedad de un ego roto. los demás, buscan sin riesgo la tranquilidad; yo, el azufre, la sustancia compulsiva y verdosa que me obsesiona. entro en ella, en el fango (lo que antes fue la nieve) y no permito que me la quiten, tampoco, frotármela, no tiene uso. apesta tanto zumo y mezcla de olor sin sentido, derramándose. no quieren revolcarse, sentir, sus ropas están bien limpias, su química pura de ser felices . . .

need crucifies you on the threshold of all perspective, and its crucifixion can't recreate your birth on the ash-covered ground where hope was left behind . . .)

. . . a hot, dark lamp outlines the shadow of my hand on the paper. scissors, I try to explain to myself the impossible duality of symbol and object: what we seem to be and what we believe ourselves to be and reality. to inscribe the memory of a time in history, to be the protagonist (agonic) of that moment, beyond its representation (without the parodies of myself in the practice of "the poetic") how to come from there, from the stairways of Leningrad, leading down from Akhmatova and the snow to me? . . . I'm sick with an incurable dream, with words that don't fulfill themselves; with creations that expand with strength, but without space, and wilt as they stack up without achieving satisfaction. the pride and sickness of a broken ego arrive as far as me. the others, they seek tranquility without running any risks; I, the sulfur, the compulsive greenish substance that I'm obsessed with. I move into the substance, the mud (which used to be snow) and I won't let them take it away from me, or scour it off of me, it has no use. it stinks, so much juice and the meaningless blending of odors, spilling. they don't want to wallow in it, they don't want to perceive, their clothes are nice and clean, the pure chemistry of their happiness . . .

la artista

. . . la música de la casa vecina es un grito remoto sobre la noche. piano mecánico: yo regreso. el balcón ha caído. estruendo de piedras sobre el fango. atónitos se miran y lo miran caer ya sin sonido, casi fantástico. una mujer ilumina con su linterna las bases desgarradas (el número de la casilla por el que reparten el sabor) la opción, me ilumina a mí y me asusto. estoy expuesta por la vidriera que ha caído desde arriba y la luz, me protejo . . .

(. . . miro una calle no menos devastada adentro. si tuviera paciencia para narrar todo aquello, cómo fue. siento pena de esos seres, que ante las frustraciones, en la fisura, buscan la ilusión, para poder saltar, sostenidos en su ingravidez por la corriente de un río sin afluentes . . . "sin los ojos del pragmatismo que evalúa la relatividad que los sostiene — dirías tú — y no su absoluto", para que nadie sintiera la verdadera corriente y sólo compensar las frustraciones, sustituir, son los desórdenes de la necesidad . . .)

. . . acelerador y freno juntos tratan de crear en nosotros una ilusión de ser, te pasas la vida así, esperando empezar, al borde. cuando termina de acabarse lo apenas comenzado y sin reflexión, la figura nos sorprende . . . esa figura soy yo que ando buscándote . . .

the artist

. . . the music from the house next door is a remote cry across the night. player piano: I return. the balcony has fallen. crash of rock on mud. astonished, people look at each other and watch it falling still without a sound, almost fantastic. with her flashlight, a woman illuminates the broken supports (the number of the window where they used to pass out spices), the choice, she trains the light on me and I get scared. I'm exposed by the light, by the glass in a window that has fallen down from above, I protect myself . . .

(. . . I see another street, no less devastated, inside me. if I were patient enough to narrate all of that, what it was like. I feel sorry for those people, faced with frustrations, who seek illusion inside the fissure, the illusion of being able to leap, of being sustained in weightlessness by the current of a river with no tributaries . . . "without the eyes of pragmatism to evaluate the relativity that supports them" — you'd say — "rather than an absolute," so no one would feel the true current and compensate only for the frustrations, to substitute, they are the disorders of necessity . . .)

. . . together, gas pedal and brake try to create in us an illusion of existing. you spend your life like that, waiting to begin, on the edge. when something hardly begun completes its ending, unreflective, the figure surprises us . . . that figure is me, out looking for you . . .

(cuando niña hacía garabatos en las libretas, todos hacíamos lo mismo. cuando alguien decía lo que yo había inventado, me quedaba perpleja y a la vez muy triste. porque todo se sabía; todo se sabía. al crecer, los garabatos — antes delirios de líneas y palabras sin descifrar — fueron conformando formas precisas, dibujos, sistemas, se había logrado la madurez, eso es, la representación, su construcción. ahora, quiero romper el dibujo consciente, su línea oscura, que me ha hecho salir de una abstracción a otra, y quiero deshacerme en aquellos garabatos del origen — no igual — porque ya aprendí el juego de hacerlos y destruirlos hasta el poder . . . los deseos dibujados son de otra especie, cuesta mucho, cuando hemos aprendido los artificiales deseos de cualquier poder, o posesión, lograr los otros . . .)

. . . una protagonista enferma de cáncer, un cangrejo crujiente. "Dulce noviembre" — aquella película donde ella satisface cada noche a un hombre diferente, hasta el amanecer, dejando en otros cuerpos su cáncer, su dolor y en cada músculo contraído, beso y muerte . . . (siempre es en la risa de la muerte que uno se suicida — dijo Edmond Jabés) . . .

(violencia de la necesidad)

. . . cáncer y mujer, no hay contradicción. termina la película, el mes, el año, el siglo, el proyecto; la era, el fin

(. . . when I was a little girl, I used to scribble in my books, we all did. when someone else spoke the words I made up, I would be perplexed, and at the same time, sad. because everything was known; everything was known. growing up, the scribbles — formerly lines of delirium and undeciphered words — took on precise forms, drawings, systems, maturity had been achieved, that's it, representation, its construction. now I want to break up the conscious drawing, its dark line, which led me from one abstraction to the other, and I want to unmake myself in those original scribbles — not the same — because I already learned to control the game of making them and destroying them . . . sketched desires are of a different breed, when we've learned the artificial desires of any power, or possession, it's hard to achieve the others . . .)

. . . a protagonist sick with cancer, a crusted crab. "Sweet November" — that movie where she satisfies a different man every night, until dawn, leaving her cancer, her pain, in other bodies and in each contracted muscle, kiss and death . . . (it's always when laughing at death that you take your own life — said Edmond Jabès) . . .

(violence of the need)

. . . cancer and woman, there's no contradiction. it's the end of the movie, the month, the year, the century, the project; the era, the end of illusion. the inner street gives

de la ilusión. la calle interior devuelve mi silueta negra también recalentada entre dos luces, sin dolor, sin olor, sin sabor, sin rencor, fantasmagórica. ficción de linterna invertida (mágica?) buscando su contenido contra el vidrio: alguna luz-brillante, momentánea, contra esa otra luz oblicua . . .

. . . "frágil, como las cosas caras, sin regreso . . ."

(plagiando a Sócrates, a Osvaldo, a mí misma, a cualquiera, con la fragilidad de llevar sencillamente una vida)

. . . ya no tengo brillo, perdí el brillo, la posibilidad del esmalte y con estas uñas, aferradas y exigiendo alguna verdad, voy perdiendo la apariencia dándole otro discurso, que ya no tiene pájaros, ni dolores de pájaros, o sombras. tal vez he sido la más ambiciosa criatura, mirándote engañar; tocando los objetos para hacer maravillas y engañandolos. detrás de la apariencia, que he perdido, ya no hay otra; detrás de esa puerta cerrada, sólo los pómulos más salientes, los huesos de la pasión que no viví, sus labios pálidos . . . (los pensamientos se desmoronan al pie de lo impensado, como pájaros al borde del cielo, escribía reb Farji) . . .

. . . cuando dejo el simulacro, la actuación, el deseo de parecer, la fábula, el plagio de un sistema de acción, dejo de ser "la artista"?

back my black silhouette, burning between two lights, without pain, without odor, without flavor, without rancor, phantasmagoric. fiction of an inverted (magic?) lamp looking for its contents in the windowpane: some light — bright, momentary, against that other, oblique light . . .

. . . "fragile, like things that are expensive, that don't come back . . ."

(plagiarizing Socrates, Osvaldo, myself, anyone, with the fragility of simply supporting a life)

. . . I don't have a glow any more, I lost the glow, the possibility of enamel and with these fingernails, holding fast and demanding some truth, I'm gradually losing my appearance while giving it another discourse, which no longer includes birds, or the sorrows of birds, or shadows. perhaps I've been the most ambitious creature, watching you deceive; touching objects to make them marvellous, deceiving them. behind the appearance, which I've lost, there's no longer any other; behind that closed door, only the most prominent cheekbones, the bones of a passion I never lived, its pale lips . . . (thoughts fall to pieces at the foot of the unthought, like birds at the edge of the sky, wrote reb Farji)

. . . when I abandon the simulacrum, the acting, the desire to seem, the fable, the plagiarism of a system of action, do I cease to be "the artist"? . . .

luz de agosto

como Lena Grove recorro las calles de Alabama y Missis-
sippi, preguntando por Lucas Burch: un hombre
desaparecido del que llevo un hijo en las entrañas. nadie
lo ha visto, o podría tener otro nombre. pero este dolor del
lado izquierdo, este pequeño ser que ha querido venir, no
lo dejará tranquilo, aunque se esconda en las cárceles del
sur . . . aún cae la lluvia, y ya no tengo leña para mantener
el fuego, ni la oración. vago despeinada y mal vestida por
la habitación del fondo, arrodillándome a cada rato contra
la lámpara de una débil angustia o luz, que parece mentir
sin prevenirnos que llegará aquel ángel de la anunciación.
y aún cae la lluvia y mis pies están fríos y enfangados.
como Lena Grove recorro también los paisajes de los
almanaques descoloridos, pasados de época, colgados de
los gigantes clavos mohosos en la pared de la cabaña mis-
erable y coloreados nuevamente en mi imaginación, en
mi terquedad de sobrevivir entre las brumas, donde los
muertos escapan ya de la incertidumbre — de esos lugares
de la existencia que fueron concebidos sin fe ni ley —.
sobreviva apenas del olvido su camisa de cuadros rojos,
sobreviva más allá de esta lluvia, hombre que finge conocer
los buenos vinos. yo como Lena Grove al final te mataré,
te mataré por haberme quitado la inocencia de no tener
ilusión nuevamente y volver donde no haya luz y

light in August

"I don't want to go where there's no light"
— *Pessoa*

like Lena Grove I walk the streets of Alabama and Missis-
sippi, asking for Lucas Burch: a man who has disappeared,
a man whose son I carry inside. no one has seen him, or
he could have another name. but this pain on my left side,
this small being who has been wanting to arrive, won't let
him alone, even if he hides in the jails of the south . . . the
rain is still falling, and I no longer have wood to keep the
fire going, or the prayer. disheveled, badly dressed, I wan-
der through the room in the back of the house, kneeling
now and then next to the lamp of a weak anguish or light,
which seems to speak lies without forewarning us that the
angel of the annunciation will arrive. and the rain still falls,
and my feet are cold and muddy. like Lena Grove, I walk
through landscapes of faded calendars, out of date, hang-
ing from the giant rusty nails on the wall of the miserable
cabin, newly colored in my imagination, by my obstinacy
of surviving in the mists, where the dead escape uncer-
tainty — from those places in existence that were conceived
without faith or law —. let his red plaid shirt barely survive
oblivion, let him survive this rain, a man who pretends to
know fine wines. like Lena Grove I will kill you at the end,
I will kill you for taking away my innocence of having no
illusions, and I will return to some place where there's no

encontraré a cualquiera que me diga que eres tú, Lucas Burch; caminaré por tu rostro menos grave y moreno, porque no puedo dejar de ser ella y perseguirte y convencerme, con este mismo hijo de los almanaques descoloridos al fondo de la habitación — la leonera — como tú la llamabas; al fondo de los vagones de tercera y de quinta, efímeros, donde los fumadores, fuman y olvidan su miseria y tantos hijos que no existirán en sus conciencias. voy saltando los charcos, mojándome los pies al borde del declive y te contemplo y te miro desde perspectivas falsas, pero tú no me ves, tú no eres de aquí: otro abismo inmediato desprende mi voluntad y me ha arrastrado hasta el charco, hacia los estragos de esa luz que hace una línea muerta en mi ojo aparente. mi ojo enrojecido por el lápiz de fingir dolor bajo mis pestañas: así parezca que he llorado por ti, Lucas Burch, y por otros.

light and I will find someone to tell me that you are you, Lucas Burch; I will walk through your dark, less serious face, because I can't stop being her and pursuing you and convincing myself, with this same child of the faded calendars in the back room — the lion-cage, as you called it; in the backs of the third- and fifth-class train cars, ephemeral, where the smokers are, they smoke and forget their misery and the many children who will never exist in their consciences. I jump over puddles as I go, getting my feet wet around the edges, and I contemplate you and I examine you from false perspectives, but you don't see me, you are not of this place: another immediate abyss unhinges my will and drags me toward the puddle, toward the ravages of the light that draws a dead line across my apparent eye. my eye, reddened by the pencil feigning pain under my eyelashes: that way it will seem as though I've cried for you, Lucas Burch, and for others.

octavo escalón

la cafetera sin tapa en medio del escalón de mármol (un escalón para cada cosa) la han dejado allí, para que yo baje a recogerla y mientras lo hago, como si sucediera infinitas veces en mí ese gesto de alzarla del frío suelo — ennegrecida por el tizne, enrojecida también — a pesar del cansancio de mis piernas que repiten el doblez de los escalones contra las corvas, uno tras otro, estalla, el movimiento de bajar y subir muchas veces repitiendo con obsesión, con placer, el mismo sentido para llegar más profundo a recogerla. qué cosa es. me veo desde abajo al tomarla así de incrédula, por la parte superior abierta y rozo con mis dedos crispándose, aquella fruta que se alza. qué alegría. llego corriendo, sé qué es. no me preguntes. no puedo responderte. deberíamos hacer una filmación sólo bajando a buscarla cada día, allí, sobre el octavo escalón de mármol, tiznada, y yo persiguiendo esa alegría de reencontrarla otra vez — no como objeto — sino como fin. ese espacio en el que hago un trayecto constante y definitivo (así pasaba el ron de una mano a la otra) así, a través del licor que se quedaba en el labio que no besa pero púrpura, tiembla, cuando la saliva se enreda y regodea en su boca sin beber, yo los observaba — aún partía las cabezas de pescado y los antiguos peces se metían en mis uñas con sus ojos (ahora pudriéndose) muertos y enrojecidos por la sal. ya no tienen visión. casi me corto para que el ron se vuelva punzante en la boca que él va a besar esta noche. cómo puede suceder. él y yo, que tantas

eighth step

coffee pot with no lid on the middle of the marble step (a
step for each thing). they left it there so I'd go down to pick
it up and while I do, as if the gesture of lifting the pot off
the cold floor were repeating infinitely — the pot black-
ened with soot, reddened as well — in spite of the exhaus-
tion of my legs, bending like the steps as they hit against
the backs of my knees, one after the other, it explodes, the
motion of descending and ascending many times, repeat-
ing obsessively, pleasurably, the same sense of arriving at
greater depths to pick up the pot. what is it. I see myself
from below as I pick it up, incredulously, by its open top
and I rub that rising fruit with my contracting fingers. what
joy. I come running, I know what it is. don't ask me. I can't
answer you. we should film just the descent every day,
there, to the eighth marble step, sooty, and me pursuing
the happiness of finding it again. — not as an object — but
as an end . . . that space in which I follow a constant and
definitive course (that's how I used to switch the rum from
one hand to the other), that's how, through the liquor left
on a lip that doesn't form a kiss but trembles, purplish,
when the saliva gets caught and rejoices in their mouths
without being swallowed, I was watching them — I was
still splitting fish heads, ancient fish got under my finger-
nails with dead and salt-reddened eyes (rotting). they've
lost their sight. I almost cut myself to make the rum turn
bitter in the mouth that he'll kiss tonight. how can it hap-
pen. he and I, who have gone down so many times to-

veces hemos bajado juntos a recoger, con el mismo sentido,
sin aroma, sin líquido, la constancia. ya sé el truco. primero
fue el arte, después de tanta reiteración, no era más que
un tono, algo pasajero, donde va a construirse el reflejo
interior de la intención (qué importa que le haya
deslumbrado la desemejanza de sus ojos acuosos). se abre
un ciclo, sangre, aparición, flores moradas: la castración.
dios incólume, escuchará la misma petición con otro
nombre (ocultamiento del sujeto) y los ángeles ladeando
sus cabezas por el asco ante el pez, algo del pecho que se
asusta y salta. el músculo, su último sitio (soy una barra
de oro en el centro de una ciudad con niebla). cuándo
conocemos bien este truco, cuándo nos acercamos a la
imagen, de qué nos sirve la oración en sus labios gruesos
quemados repitiéndola? has matado el recurso, para
volverlo a poseer. ella en mí. nada, ni una mancha de
sangre alrededor. voluntad. puedo cortarme ahora con este
cuchillo para que el pez me mate y en vez de sábanas
blancas, luces purísimas, para alumbrar el espectáculo que
has hecho, sean verdes cobertores de hospital, algo
siniestro y yo, ridícula como siempre y al fin, de qué servirá
la fetidez de los cadáveres que hemos abrazado? de una
solución? continuamente olía a musgo, puedo cambiar
todavía el sentido, pero para qué? la cafetera sin asa ya,
sin tapa, está en mi mano. no es una reliquia, ni tiene más
historia que ese borde de cansancio donde se asienta tanto
líquido y humedad. está mustia, bajo un tenue gris tiznado
sobre el mármol. hierática es una obra perfecta, ausente,

gether, with the same meaning, without scent, without liq-
uid, constancy. now I know the trick. first came the art,
after so much reiteration, it was nothing more than a tone,
something fleeting, where the internal reflection of inten-
tion was going to be constructed (what does it matter that
the dissimilarity of their watery eyes has dazzled him). a
cycle begins, blood, apparition, purple flowers: castration.
harmless, god will hear the same petition under another
name (masking of the subject) and angels tilt their heads
in disgust at the fish, something from the breast that takes
fright and leaps, the muscle, its last place (I'm a gold bar in
the center of a foggy city). when will we know this trick
well, when will we get close to the image, what good does
it do us, image with a prayer on its thick, burned lips, re-
peating? you've killed the option off now to use it later. the
prayer in me. nothing, not a bloodstain anywhere. deter-
mination. I can cut myself now with this knife so the fish
will kill me and instead of white sheets, the purest lights,
to illuminate the spectacle you've made, there will be green
hospital scrubs, something sinister and I, ridiculous as usual
and in the end, what will be the good of the cadaverous
stench we've embraced? will it be a solution? it always
smelled of moss, I can still change the meaning, but for
what? the coffeepot missing its handle, missing its lid, is in
my hand. it's not a relic, it has no history other than that
edge of exhaustion where so much liquid and humidity
settle. it's faded, under a small gray stain on the marble.
hieratical, it's a perfect work, absent, without context, with-

sin contexto, sin recuerdo, sin dolor. y rígida, no ha podido quemarme: existe para colocar mi propio dolor en un rincón: mi exceso de soberbia, mi vanidad, mi obsesión de fingir. su humo gris que late y regocija en mí la dicotomía (la vuelvo a recoger para que me de su trayecto y no olvide una ceremonia cualquiera). literaturizo, tienes razón. la poesía — de esa se hablará cuando termine de pitar con fuerza, casi con fiebre — será otra cosa. no el tiempo de recogerla en el acto de bajar, subir, apresar, un recorrido. la poesía . . . es ya no verla. saber que no la necesito, que no vuelvo por ella; que me es innecesaria esta búsqueda laberíntica del sentir. no tiene fin, ni recuerdo. (como tu frase, amor, amor, qué te pasa . . .) suena y rompe, en el abrupto camino, contra los ojos de los pescados nauseabundos que miran cortar esas cabezas truncadas (porque no puedo otras) y antes fueron iniciados para vivir como peces, o como ángeles. ella me está mirando balancearme con el cuchillo en la mano y fingir otra vez, que corto cabezas muertas porque no obtengo otro espacio dentro del sueño cóncavo y sin anestesia, del cual voy despertando cómplice y no me alivia — tendría que matar. en los más profundo, siento el silbido y un olor a través de la noche y junto al olor, agrietándose, junto a la fetidez, algo que empieza a corromperse con el término de todo fin.

out memory, without pain. and, rigid, it hasn't managed to burn me: it exists in order to locate my own pain in a corner: my excess of pride, my vanity, my obsession with pretense. its gray smoke that throbs and rejoices about the dichotomy in me (I go back to pick it up so it will give its course to me and I won't forget just any ceremony). I'm making it literature, you're right. poetry — they'll speak of it when it stops whistling forcefully, almost feverishly — it will be something else. not the time needed to pick it up in the act of descending, ascending, clutching, a journey. poetry . . . is to not see it any more. to know that I don't need it, that I'm not going back for it; that this labyrinthine search for feeling is unnecessary to me. it has no end or memory. (like your phrase, darling, darling, what's wrong . . .) it sounds and it breaks, on the short path, against the eyes of those loathsome fish watching me slice into decapitated heads (because I can't stand others), and before, they were created to live like fish, or like angels. it's watching me sway with the knife in my hand, I'm pretending again that I cut into dead heads because I have no other space within the concave and unanesthetized dream, from which I keep waking up an accomplice, without relief — I'd have to kill. at the greatest depth, I hear the whistle blow and I smell an odor in the night and along with the odor, splitting, along with the stench, I sense something that begins to spoil with the completion of all purpose.

ski sauvage

. . . hay una choza por una montaña. la espuma del cielo da a
la montaña un cerco traslúcido y fresco. el aire alrededor de la
montaña es sonoro, piadoso, legendario, prohibido. la entrada
a la montaña está prohibida. la montaña tiene su lugar en el
alma. es el horizonte de algo y retrocede sin cesar, da una
sensación de eterno horizonte . . . y yo describo esa pintura con
lágrimas, porque esta pintura golpea mi corazón, siente como
mi pensamiento se despliega en ella, en un espacio ideal,
absoluto, pero en un espacio que tendría una forma
incorporable a la realidad. allí caigo del cielo . . .
— Artaud

la línea negra (más abrupta) es la que rompe nuestro
equilibrio con esos saltos que nos desvían de lo continuo.
tú preferías la roja. porque, como yo, era un río de sangre
que se teme y arrebata. nos permitía continuar sobre las
botas hacia un declive tenue — deslizarse y fingir — que
rompemos las bolsas de aire con el pulmón y abrimos con
el cuerpo encarnado la ilusión de una forma. alados, sobre
el inmenso blanco que se hace púrpura-azul con la
desesperación del después. después de este amor? después
de este mar? después de esta metáfora? . . . deslizarse y
caer sobre la nieve espumosa, bañándonos de luz, de
champang, de algas rojas . . . tanto hemos sufrido de querer
abrir la línea límite del objeto, del sentimiento, de la
palabra, el borde. el borde de la naturaleza es negro y nos
descerebramos en un intento de atravesar (los cielos donde

ski sauvage

there's a cabin on a mountain. the sky's foam gives the mountain a cool, transparent atmosphere. the air around the mountain is sonorous, pious, legendary, prohibited. the entrance to the mountain is prohibited. the mountain has its place in the soul. it's the horizon of something and it retreats ceaselessly. it gives the sensation of an eternal horizon . . . and I describe that painting with tears, because this painting strikes my heart. it feels how my thought unfurls across the canvas, a space that's ideal, absolute, but a space with a form that could be incorporated into reality. there I fall out of the sky . . .
— Artaud

the black line (more abrupt) ruptures our equilibrium with those skips that cause us to deviate from continuity. you preferred the red line. because, like me, it was a fearsome river of blood — it could wash you away. it allowed us to keep going along in our boots toward a tenuous slope — to glide and to pretend — that we rupture air pockets with our lungs and open, with our bodies incarnate, the illusion of a form. swift, across the immense whiteness that turns purple-blue with the desperation of the after. after this love? after this ocean? after this metaphor? to glide and to fall on the frothy snow, bathing ourselves in light, in champagne, in red algae . . . we've suffered so much from wanting to open up the line at the edge of the object, the feeling, the word, the border. nature's border is black and we'll brain ourselves in an attempt to cross it (the skies where

nos suicidábamos al revés, hacia la infinitud, contra la gravedad). las colinas ensangrentadas bajo la nieve en pico que me ha cortado la pierna izquierda al rozar y yo, más que sufrir la herida, describo su dolor (estética) del desastre. contra toda protección — desprotegidos — mirando la fisura en el espejo por donde sangro, primero oliendo, tocando la burbuja que nace y después, siempre mirar desde esta altura cómplice el cuerpo empequeñecido y oscuro del acto en el que hemos participado como suceso, no como elección, de las diferentes líneas de fuga hemos tomado una como camino — no como fin — y esta línea roja y lírica nos permite concentrar las sensaciones en la estructura de un sentimiento; latir con la explosión de una palabra (envoltura) que encubra y proteja nuestro deseo. la poesis de esta línea acuosa, me permite fingir que este paisaje humano es de nieve. y está adentro. sin la distancia del (mi) intermediario, la asumo como un (yo). pero me canso del dibujo y lo lanzo (la bota salta y suelta su mecanismo del patín y no caigo). existe una diferencia, o el ser está en la diferencia? así puedo repetir incesante la caída. pero el espacio va y viene, la escritura se aleja de sí misma (el movimiento del trazo entra en el propio movimiento del texto) de la vida? la diferencia es opción. no existe la diferencia en el centro (cada cosa es la misma cosa). la diferencia es periférica y me gusta vagar, rajar esos bordes oblicuos que parecen determinar alguna estructura del sentimiento entre esas pistas de complejidad

we used to commit suicide in reverse, toward infinity, against gravity). the bloodstained hills under the snowy peak that cut into my left leg when I scraped against it and I, rather than suffering from the wound, describe its pain (aesthetics) of disaster. against all protection — unprotected — looking in the mirror at the fissure from which I bleed, first sniffing, touching the bubble that appears and later, from that accomplice height, to always watch the body, shrunken and dark from the act in which we've participated as an incident, not as a choice. of the different lines of escape, we've chosen one as a means — not as an end — and this red, lyric line allows us to concentrate our sensations inside the structure of a feeling, to throb with the explosion of a word (wrapper) that encloses and protects our desire. the poesis of this watery line allows me to pretend that this human landscape is one of snow. and it's inside. without the difference of the (my) intermediary, I assume it as an (I). but I'm tired of the drawing and I throw it away (the boot bucks and drops its binding and I don't fall). does a difference exist, or is the self in the difference? that's how I can repeat the fall incessantly. but the space comes and goes. does the writing move away from itself (the motion of the stroke enters the very motion of the text), from life? the difference is choice. the difference doesn't exist at the center (each thing is the same thing). the difference is peripheral and I like to wander, to split those oblique borders that seem to determine some structure of feeling between trails of complexity that the artist chooses

que el artista escoge para su azul, su verde, su negra gravedad. las pistas no están en el contexto, sólo hacen la mediación entre el interior y la superficie blanquísima del monte (su página). Mont Blanc como fin y muerte. y la metáfora (pisapapel con nieve hecha de trigo blanco que se voltea sin derretirse) es la ficción verdadera. todo hombre está solo en su determinación. y ésta no es más que el tono que le agrede al elegir en el tiempo. no en el espacio, su espacio, que es instante y repetición. lo hemos sentido desde alturas diferentes (los frailejones amarillos parecen bosques, como nosotros pretendemos sombras de árboles). sobre el parecer de esta realidad, una fijeza: estamos presos entre el aire gris del pisapapel, sus pinos verdes y ese borde que es cielo y es cristal. de ahí la fábula; la oración que se construye para salvarnos de no regresar del hueco negro, su línea oscura, el punto de fuga de mayor peligrosidad (mi discurso femenino es sintaxis; engrapamiento del tejido en el que atrapo a la noche). la campana da el sonido último con horror, se abre y es mi momento fatal de intervenir, de deslizarme asustada (crear en nosotros espacios de vida, espacios que no existían, que no parecían poder encontrar sitio en el espacio). ustedes esperaban una historia. atrévanse a discernir si han cabalgado sobre un ski sauvage, entre el ocio y la suavidad de esa caricia con franjas de obsenidad que es la escritura.

for his blue, his green, his black gravity. the trails aren't in the context, they just mediate the interior and the white surface of the mountain (his page). Mont Blanc as end and death. and the metaphor (paperweight with snow made from blanched wheat that whirls around without melting) is the real fiction. every man is alone in his determination. and this is nothing more than the tone that assaults him when he makes a choice in time. not in space, his space, which is instant and repetition. we've sensed it at different heights (the yellow espeletia seem like forests, as we court shadows of trees). over the appearance of this reality, a fixity: we're imprisoned between the gray air of the paperweight, its green pines, and the border that is the sky and is made of glass. from here, the fable: the sentence constructed to save ourselves from not coming back from the black hole, its dark line, the most dangerous point of escape. (my feminine discourse is syntax; stapling of the tapestry in which I capture the night). the bell sounds its last peal with horror, it opens and that's my fatal moment to intervene, to glide, frightened (to create inside us spaces for life, spaces that didn't exist, that didn't seem to be able to find a location in space). you were expecting a story. dare to discern whether you've ridden on a *ski sauvage*, between the leisure and that soft caress, with streaks of the obscenity that is writing.

la obra

tomamos el té, corriente, bajo la lámpara art-nouveau, de
imitación. alrededor del centro de la mesa están reunidos:
el teólogo, el astrólogo, el crítico, el investigador, el hippy,
el productor, la funcionaria, el arquitecto, el ingeniero, la
bailarina, el escritor, el perro dálmata, el editor, la guionista,
una pintora, el director y los cantantes. nadie se ha situado
fuera de la luz, los claros y oscuros del vidrio de fingir . . .
"como mercurio resbalando, como limaduras de hierro
atraídas por el imán, los distraídos se unieron. la música
comenzó; la primera nota comportaba la segunda; la
segunda, la tercera. luego en la superficie nació una fuerza
en oposición, después otra. divergían a distintos niveles . . ."
cada uno necesita de su representación para subsistir, de
diferente manera, pero en conjunto discriminados del
centro: el teólogo enseña a dios: es el lugar donde él cree
no ser discriminado por los hombres; el astrólogo prepara
su carta natal y augura hasta su plato del porvenir, no me
burlo. todos serios en sus puestos aspiran a alguna verdad,
a alguna conciencia de su tránsito (una cosa útil para la
vida implica una cosa que lleva a cada ser a preservar en
el ser, según la exposición de Spinoza) todos quieren hacer
prevalecer su servidumbre como un medio, o un poder
contra la muerte. ellos quisieron expresar alguna cosa.
ninguno vio los cielos transparentes, alguna estrella, la
producción final en medio de la danza . . . "a distintos
niveles nosotros avanzamos; cogiendo algunas flores de
la superficie; descendiendo otros para luchar con el

100

the work

we're sipping tea, as usual, under the imitation art nouveau lamp, they're gathered around the center of the table: the theologian, the astrologer, the critic, the researcher, the hippie, the producer, the functionary, the architect, the engineer, the dancer, the writer, the dalmatian dog, the editor, the screenwriter, a painter, the director and the singers. no one has taken a place outside the light, the brights and darks in the window of pretense: "like mercury sliding, like iron filings attracted by the magnet, the distracted people joined the group. the music began; the first note led to the second; the second to the third. then on the surface an opposing force was born, then another. they diverged at different levels . . ." they all need their own personal representations to survive, in different ways, but as a group separated from the center: the theologian teaches god — it's the place, he believes, where men don't discriminate against him; the astrologer prepares his chart and predicts even his next meal, I'm not joking. taking their positions seriously, they all aspire to some truth, to some consciousness of their motion (something useful for life implies something that leads each being toward preservation in the self, according to Spinoza). all of them want to make their servitude prevail as a medium, or as a power to ward off death. they tried to express something. none of them saw the transparent heavens, any star, the final production in the middle of the dance . . . "we advance to different levels; some plucking flowers at the surface; others

significado; pero todos comprendiendo; todos incorporados." cuánto insecto roto, quemado en esa lámpara, bajo esa luz de atraer sólo a los comejenes, intensos voladores que aspiran llegar al sol, a la claridad, para morirse luego encerrados allí, al final último de una luz mediocre . . . "como mercurio resbalando, como limaduras de hierro atraídas por el imán . . ." los amigos inteligentes y esta tristeza de verlos como son bajo el fuego de sus intenciones mediatas, de sus intereses menores y empañados por el reflejo verdoso, por la imitación de una lámpara sin estilo, ¡mis pequeños, mis frágiles amigos! me aferro, se ahogan, me ahogan, me agarro al cisne en perfil sobre el fondo del cuadro, lo hundo más. la bailarina pone su pie desnudo sobre la mesa, lo dobla y dorado lo contrae. habrá otra oportunidad para mí, para ellos? cómo saber quién soy despojada de lo que parece que soy, de lo que por momentos pretendo ser, de los que algunas veces sueño? y ellos, recortados entre índice y pulgar, son una entelequia, también? estoy desaparecida bajo un cono de luz posterior y apenas me ven. cómo resolver la capacidad de la emoción y el sentir infinito, si la expresión es poca, sólo son las palabras, esas pequeñas quemaduras que hacen manchas en las alas bajitas? no existe la obra, ya no existe la obra . . . "porque toda la población de la inmensa profundidad de la mente llegó en tropel; procedente de lo carente de protección, de lo despellejado; y vino el alba; el azul del caos y la cacofonía . . . la medida.

descending to wage war on the meaning; but all of us understanding; all of us included." how many crushed insects, burnt in that lamp, beneath that light which attracts only termites, intense fliers who aspire to reach the sun, to achieve clarity, to die then, enclosed there, at the last ending of a mediocre light . . . "like mercury sliding, like iron filings attracted by the magnet . . ." the intelligent friends and this sorrow of seeing them as they are under the flame of their half-fulfilled intentions, the flame of their minor interests tarnished by the greenish reflection, by the imitation of a lamp of no style at all, my small, my fragile friends! I hold fast, they drown, they drown me, I grab onto the profile of a swan in the corner of the painting, I pull it further under. the dancer rests her bare foot on the table, she flexes it and contracts it, golden. will there be another chance for me, for them? how can I know who I am, stripped of what I seem to be, of what I try to be moment by moment, of what I sometimes dream? and they, silhouetted between index finger and thumb, are they an entelechy too? I've disappeared under a cone of light behind them and they hardly see me. how do I sort out the capacity for emotion and the infinite feeling, if the expression is limited, it's only words, little burn marks spotting the lower wings? the work does not exist, the work does not exist anymore . . . "because the entire population of the mind's immense depths arrived in a tumbling rush; coming from an absence of protection, from the removal of the skin; and dawn came, the blue of chaos and cacophony . . . the

convocados desde el borde de horrorosos abismos; chocaban; se avenían; se unían. algunos relajaron los dedos de las manos; y otros descruzaban las piernas . . ." has visto al final sus gestos, la perduración de sus gestos semiborrados entre la luz de la noche que avanza y el terror del amanecer que se aproxima buscando por qué ventana entrar a la representación y someterlo a sus rostros, a los rostros que no fueron? es el instante de no esperar más y recoger las cenizas, los restos del cigarro incesante en los dedos prácticos de ella que vigila, se aproxima y espera, otra vibración aparente: todo pasa porque debieron elegir, porque estamos siempre eligiendo, moviendo las antenas y no hay por qué en las elecciones a la altura de nuestra intuición: el director lo sabe. los momentos son claves, no tienen espacio ni tiempo, pero tampoco definen algo más allá de nuestra elección fallida, presionada por miles de resortes ajenos, sólo un movimiento falso de la antena . . . "como limaduras de hierro atraídas por el imán . . ." tú puedes defenderme de mí? del círculo estrecho de una vida, un destino, sus horarios, una complicidad? podrás convocar el lugar — no el país — donde este cono se abra en mi interior hacia otra experiencia entre la tranquilidad y el desasosiego? el productor mira con ojos pálidos y se levanta: un lugar para un sueño, un espacio para un vivo que no puede existir vulnerable y humano con el único enemigo que podría hacerlo olvidar: la realidad. tú podrás con las botas y el

measure. brought from the border of abysmal horrors, they crashed together; they reconciled; they united. some relaxed the fingers on their hands; and others uncrossed their legs . . ." in the end, you've seen their gestures, the duration of their partially erased gestures between the light of the advancing nightfall and the terror of the dawn, which approaches in search of a window through which it can enter the show and throw itself into their faces, into the faces that didn't go? it's the instant for waiting no longer, for collecting the ashes, the remains of the perpetual cigarette in the practical fingers of the woman who keeps watch, the sun approaches and waits, another apparent vibration. everything happens because they should have made a choice, because we are always choosing, waving our antennae and there's no reason in those choices that's as lofty as our intuition: the director knows it. the moments are key, they have no space or time, but neither do they define anything beyond our failed choice, pressured by thousands of faraway mechanisms, just one false move of an antenna . . . "like iron filings attracted to the magnet . . ." can you defend me from myself? from the narrow circle of a life, a destiny, its schedules, a complicity? will you be able to summon the place — not the country — where this cone inside me could open out into another experience between tranquility and anxiety? the producer looks on with pale eyes, and gets up: a place for a dream, a space for a living man who can't coexist, vulnerable and human, with the only enemy that could make him forget: reality. with

morral construir ese jardín para las flores, edificar esa jerarquéa . . . comiendo algunas flores de la superficie; descendiendo otros para luchar con el significado . . . tú podrás? hay por qué? mientras, se va cerrando el tiempo, el espacio que te tocó concebir. tomamos té, corriente, bajo la lámpara art-nouveau de imitación verdadera. alrededor del centro, el silencio no tiene piedad con los que esperan. es un sonámbulo más de esta noche, que dormido se lanza por el balcón hacia el muelle: con el silencio no es la magia lo que se destruye, sino el símbolo . . . es otra forma de perderse, un pausa, la medida . . . "solamente dominada por la melodía del sonido superficial; también por los guerreros de emplumados cascos de guerra que guerreaban para separarse . . . obligados por la llamada de los confines del horizonte . . ." se averiaron nuestras alas antes de ver la luz y era un vuelo muy largo de seres humanos, no de arcángeles; hacia la realidad más real, hacia la imagen de lo real. puede uno permanecer mucho tiempo en la imagen de lo real. es el final de la obra.

your boots and your knapsack you can build that garden for the flowers, construct that hierarchy . . . eating some flowers at the surface; others descending to wage war on the meaning . . . will you be able to do it? is there a reason to do it? meanwhile, time closes in upon itself, space that it's your turn to conceive. we're drinking tea, as usual, under the art nouveau lamp that's a true imitation. around the center, the silence has no pity for those who wait, it's one more sleepwalker tonight who jumps off the balcony toward the dock while sleeping: with the silence it's not the magic that's destroyed, but the symbol . . . it's another way of getting lost, a pause, the measure . . . "only dominated by the melody of the superficial sound, and by the warriors with plumed war helmets who waged war for separation . . . compelled by the call of the horizon's confines . . ." our wings were damaged before we saw light and it was a long flight of humans, not of archangels; toward the most real reality, toward the image of the real. one can stay a long time in the image of the real. it's the end of the work.

la isla de Wight

yo era como aquella chica de las isla de Wight
— el poema no estaba terminado
era el centro del poema lo que nunca estaba terminado
ella había buscado
desesperadamente
ese indicio de la arboladura.
había buscado . . .
hasta no tener respuestas ni preguntas
y ser lo mismo que cualquiera
bajo esa indiferencia de la materia
a su necesidad. el yo se agrieta.
(un yo criminal y lúdico que la abraza
a través de los pastos ocres y resecos del verano)
ella había buscado la infinitud azul del universo en el
    ser.
— lo que dicen gira en torno a sus primeros años
cuando el padre murió sin haber tenido demasiado
conocimiento del poema —
sé que esa mentira que ha buscado
obtiene algún sentido al derretirse
en sus ojos oscuros. ha buscado el abrupto sentido del
    sentir
que la rodea.
(un poema es lo justo, lo exacto, lo irrepetible,
dentro del caos que uno intenta ordenar y ser)
y lo ha ordenado para que el poema no sea necesario.

Isle of Wight

I was like that girl from the Isle of Wight
— the poem wasn't finished
it was the middle of the poem that was never finished
she had searched
desperately
for some sign of the ship on the horizon.
she had searched . . .
until she had neither answers nor questions
and was the same as anyone else
under matter's indifference
to her need. the I cracks.
(a criminal and ludic I who embraces her
through dry, ochre, summer grasses)
she had searched for the universe's blue infinity in the
    self.
— what they say revolves around her early years
when her father died without knowing too much
about the poem —
I know that the lie she's been looking for
gathers meaning when it melts
inside her dark eyes. she has looked for the abrupt sense
    of sensing
that surrounds her.
(a poem is the precise thing, the accurate thing, the
    unrepeatable thing
within the chaos that one tries to arrange and be)
and she has arranged it so the poem won't be necessary.

despojada del poema y de mi
va buscando con su pasión de perseguir
la cualidad. ha perdido, ha buscado.
ha contrapuesto animales antagónicos que han venido a
   morir
bajo mi aparente neutralidad de especie
un gato, un pez, un pájaro . . . sólo provocaciones.
— te digo que los mires —
para hallar otra cosa entre esa línea demoledora de las
   formas
que chocan al sentir su resonancia.
también aquí se trata del paso del tiempo,
de la travesía del mar por el poema —
adonde ellos iban, los poemas no habían llegado
   todavía.
yo era como aquella chica de la isla de Wight
había buscado en lo advenidizo
la fuga y la permanencia de lo fijo y me hallo
dispuesta a compartir con ella a través de las tachaduras
si el poema había existido alguna vez materialmente
si había sido escrito ese papel
para conservar el lugar de una espera.

stripped of the poem and of me
she goes on looking with her passion for pursuing a
quality. she has lost, she has searched.
she has counterposed antagonistic animals that have
    come to die
under my apparent neutrality with regard to species
a cat, a fish, a bird . . . only provocations.
— I'm telling you to look at them —
to find something else in that devastating line of shapes
that collide when they sense their resonance.
here too it deals with the passage of time,
with the ocean travelling through the poem —
wherever they were going, the poems hadn't yet arrived.
I was like that girl from the Isle of Wight
I had searched in what was fleeting
for an escape and the permanence of what was secure
    and I find myself
disposed to let her know through the corrections
whether the poem had existed materially at any time
whether that paper had been written
to preserve a place for waiting.

dos veces son el mínimo

aquí media luz; afuera, la mañana.
miro por la abertura de la media negra
que hace un ángulo exacto con mi pie que está
arriba. un mundo que me interesa
aparece por la cicatriz; un deseo que me interesa
rehusando la prudencia.
los ruidos bajo el sol entrada la mañana.
por la abertura en triángulo del muslo hasta el pie en tu
    boca
hay un canal
la total ausencia de intención de este día,
un día en que uno se expone y luego enferma.
un día formando un gran arco entre el dedo que roza
el labio y la media.
dos veces son el mínimo de confianza
para lograr la ilusión. yo, al amanecer,
estaba junto a la ventana (era la única imagen
en la que podría refugiarme) me acercaba para no llegar
y estar convencida — nunca reafirmada —
"como si, para mí, tú, la otra, te abrieras, o te rompieras,
del modo más suave contra el alféizar."
(las palabras siempre son de algún otro, se prestan
para consolar a la sensación que también
viene de allá afuera, incontrolable) otra cosa
es lo que you hago con ellas aquí adentro:

twice is the minimum

here half-light; outside, the morning.
I look out of the half-dark's opening
that forms a precise angle with my foot
up there. a world that interests me
appears through the scar; a desire that interests me
refusing prudence.
noise under the mid-morning sun.
through the triangular opening from my thigh to my foot
   inside your mouth
there's a channel
the complete absence of intention today,
a day to expose oneself and then fall ill.
a day forming a great arc between my stocking and
the finger that grazes my lip.
twice is the minimum for trust
to achieve the illusion. at dawn I
was next to the window (the only image
in which I could hide) I came close but wouldn't arrive
at being convinced — never reaffirmed —
"as if, for me, you, the other woman, opened up, or
   broke,
in the gentlest way against the windowsill."
(the words always belong to someone else, they lend
   themselves
to consoling the feeling that also
comes from out there, uncontrollable) something else
is what I do with them here inside:

las caliento escuchando bien un sonido que me revela la
     tonalidad
de lo que expongo (una ilusión) de ser aquella
que algo dio en el triángulo cuya cúspide es tu boca
absorbiendo también de la sustancia.
yo sólo me aproximaba a la ventana
— escritora nómada — que mira con devoción
en vez de coger a ciegas (la primera vez) sabe que
dos veces son el mínimo de vida de ser.
júrame que no saldremos del "territorio del poema" esta
     vez
que si estrujo y pierdo en el cesto de los papeles
este cuerpo
no voy a renacer al espectáculo. estamos juntos
en el diseño con tinta de un día que no es verdadero
porque osa comprimirse en la línea del encanto.
— de la cintura hacia arriba está la carne, el día.
de la mitad inferior de tronco (abajo) media negra hasta
la noche, el fin.
júrame que no saldremos de aquí
una casa prestada con ventanas que miran hacia el mar
     de papel
donde nos desnudamos, rodamos, prestamos, palabras
     para lavar
volver a teñir en el crepúsculo. era mi cuerpo ese
promontorio que tú colocabas al derecho, al revés,
sobre el piso de mármol?
fue esa tumba siempre, los ojillos de los poros

I warm them listening carefully to a sound that reveals
   the tonality
of what I expose (an illusion), of being that woman
who gave something, in the triangle with its apex at your
   mouth,
getting something from the substance as well.
I was just approaching the window
— nomadic writer — who looks on devotedly
instead of grasping blindly (the first time) and knows that
twice is the minimum you can live.
swear to me that we won't leave "the poem's territory"
   this time
that if I crumple up and lose this body
in the wastebasket
I won't be reborn into the spectacle. we're together
in the inked design of an untrue day
because it dares to compress itself in lines of pleasure.
— from the waist up is the flesh, the day.
— from the lower half of the torso (down) darkened to
the night, the end.
swear to me we won't leave this place
a house on loan with windows opening to the sea of
   paper
where we undress, roll, lend words to wash
to make more stains in the dark. was it my body, that
promontory you pointed toward you, then away from you,
on the marble floor?
was it always that tomb, the pores' openings

como gusanos olfateando mis pensamientos
para nada?
yo siempre quise ver lo que tú mirabas
por la abertura del triángulo
(ser los dos a la vez) algo doble en el mismo sitio
de los cuerpos y en los pies, longitudes distintas
"para aquel contacto de una suavidad maravillosa."

dos veces son el mínimo de vida de ser.
yo, una vez más, ensayo la posibilidad de renacer
(de la posteridad ya no me inquieta nada).

like worms aimlessly sniffing out
my thoughts?
I always tried to see what you were seeing
through the triangular opening
(to be the two at once) something double in the same
    place
as the bodies, and something double in the feet, different
    lengths,
"for that contact of a marvellous gentleness."

twice is the minimum you can live.
I test the possibility of rebirth
(nothing about posterity worries me any more).

Can I be God?

PARA SILVIA PLATH

(cada día es una plegaria renovada para que dios exista
para que me visite con mayor fuerza y claridad.)
— S P

la amiga de Alicia, una amiga mía, vivió en Inglaterra.
— la amiga de mi amiga Alicia, no la del cuento —
conoció a un hombre que hacia pastar su rebano
cerca de la cabaña donde Silvia y Ted
habían tenido a su segundo hijo. ella lo invitó a un trago
— muy eufórica —
y el hombre que no sabía nada de poesía
sólo recordaba que Silvia era
una mujer que caminaba sola por los páramos
al atardecer.
no conozco a la amiga de mi amiga,
pero alargando ese final
encuentro una nota con su foto — al fondo —
y le agradezco ese trago de vino donde
echó sus palabras hacia el atardecer,
que además de traernos el mes de abril
las islitas de sílabas con un poco de color
donde sobresalen preguntas sin respuestas a Dios
(Dear God, can I be God?)
vuelven a mirar la sonrisa pendiente
de un milagro. la blanca espuma de la leche

Can I be God?

FOR SYLVIA PLATH

(each day renews a prayer that god exists,
that he will visit with increased force and clarity.)
— S. P.

Alice's friend, a friend of mine, lived in England.
my friend Alice — not Alice from the story — her friend
met a man who sent his flock to graze
near the cabin where Sylvia and Ted
had their second child. she invited him over for a drink
— euphoric —
and the man who knew nothing about poetry
only remembered that Sylvia was
a woman who walked alone across the moors
at sundown.
I don't know my friend's friend,
but extending that ending
I find a note on the bottom of her photo
and I thank her for the glass of
wine in which she threw her words at the setting sun,
bringing us the month of April
with a touch of color where unanswered questions for
    God
appear *(Dear God, can I be God?)* and
little syllabic islands form the dangling smile
of a miracle. milk's white foam

para que se enfríe
junto al sol naranja de sus ojos prendidos en el horno
Silvia y Ted tenían una casita
en el atardecer de los páramos
cubierta por plantas túpidas y tallos muy altos
donde uno (a la luz del atardecer
cree que todo es posible;
incluso convertirse in Dios).
ella se levantaba muy temprano
y vomitaba con horror su imposibilidad
— la retama roja y amarilla —
dentro de una palabra de cristal
que pujaba y pujaba sin poder jamás
convertirse en él
(una afirmación como un latigazo. Dios).
era una niña desaliñada
que conoció a la Sra. Davies
y a la Sra. Plum y al comandante Crump,
pero que no podía convertirse en Dios
pero que podía creer en él
pero que no podía saltar sobre su otra religión
y caer al abismo
sin artificialidad alguna.
y el hombre que en tiempos de Plath
haciá pacer su rebaño cerca de la cabaña
lo concentró todo en el cuenco de vino
en la espuma de leche
en el fuego naranja del zorro que sabía,

grows cold alongside the orange light of her eyes,
    glowing from the oven.
Sylvia and Ted had a little house
in the sunset on the moors
it was covered by thick plants and tall stalks
where she (in the dusky light)
believed that everything was possible,
even becoming God.
she used to rise very early
and vomit her impossibility with horror
— red and yellow furze —
within a crystal word
that struggled and struggled without ever
becoming him
(statement like a whiplash. God).
she was a slovenly girl
who met Mrs. Davies
and Mrs. Plum and Major Crump,
but who couldn't change into God
but who could believe in him
but who couldn't leap over her other religion
and fall into the abyss
without some artificiality,
and the man who in Plath's times
sent his flock to graze near the cabin
concentrated on the bowl of wine,
on the milk's foam,
on the orange flame of the fox that knew

cómo abandonaría el cuerpo de la muchacha
exactamente a la hora especificada
porque, aunque la paciente parecía poseída,
su mal no era posesión, sino la emoción
del remordimiento por no poder convertirse en Dios
(ni a Ted, ni a su padre, ni a su madre, ni a sus amigos,
    en Dios).
y así perdió el sentido de su individualidad
hacia el atardecer, de un morado increíblemente
intenso como el vino
en la casita, que no era una cabaña sino un templo
para su crucifixión
donde la amiga de mi amiga Alicia — no la del cuento —
la vio a través de los ojos de Dios
la última vez.

how he would abandon the girl's body
exactly at the specified hour
because, although the patient seemed possessed,
her evil was not possession but the emotion
of guilt for being incapable of becoming God
(incapable of turning Ted, or her father, or her mother, or
    her friends, into God).
and in this guilt she lost herself
until nightfall, a purple incredibly
intense like wine
in the little house, which was not a cabin but a temple
for her crucifixion
where my friend Alice's friend — not Alice from the story
    — this friend
saw her through the eyes of God
the last time.

un caballero tracio

un caballero tracio del siglo II me contempla
desde el relieve votivo
donde alguien lo petrificó
sobre el caballo. Oh Plutonio! condenado eternamente
yo digo el salmo de tu destino cercano, yo toco
los arabescos carcomidos y espoleados al sol en su
    venganza.
(la sierpe observa a la derecha cualquier movimiento
para saltar si te equivocas y enroscarte)
pero sólo asusta a los insectos que mordisquean
las frutas que el caballo reventó contra el fango.
ha pasado un segundo antes de tu muerte
y la sonrisa de bronce y plomo
deja un sabor ocre en mis labios. te he besado
contra el papel moderno de la fotografía
y nos hemos confundido en ese instante
donde me quedo en ti
donde vienes con tu destino cercano tras un rostro
    antiguo
y yo hago la escritura de mi boca en la piedra.
¿de dónde provienen tantas cosas que antes fuimos
aquí — ahora?

a Thracian rider

a Thracian rider from the second century watches me
from the relief
where someone turned him to stone
on top of his horse. Oh Plutonius! eternally condemned
I recite the psalm of your approaching destiny, I touch
arabesques, worm-eaten and spurred toward the sun in
    vengeance.
(from the right, the serpent observing your movements
will jump out and coil around you if you make a mistake)
but it only frightens insects nibbling on
the fruits that the rider breaks open in the mud.
it happened an instant before your death
the bronzed and leadened smile
leaves ochre on my lips. I kissed your photograph
on its modern paper
and in that instant we became confused
I remain in you
you come with your approaching destiny behind an
    ancient face
and I trace my mouth's writing on rock.
where do they come from, so many things that we once
    were,
here — now?

perdí una palabra

. . . perdí una palabra que me buscaba . . .
una palabra en la que de buen grado te perdí.
— P. Celán

la palabra con la que uno camina se adelanta
a lo que uno camina. y uno ya es esa palabra
con una braza por delante a lo que viene detrás
que es el cuerpo . . . un volumen, un ademán,
aislado de su palabra que le abre paso sin que pierda el
    sentido
de ocupar el lugar de la palabra. una fortificación.
esta mañana ella me despertó
antes de mover los dedos, las pestañas, la brisa para
    sofocar
mi huevo y su luminosidad; para saciar un poco
el hambre de adelantarme a mí, retrocediendo,
sin encontrar un cuerpo que soporte su majestuosidad,
el derroche de sílabas repletas de labios
en el éter de pronunciar la redondez que habla del
    contorno
y provoca al fin esa palabra. (porque el gato tiene
dieciséis mutilaciones de palabras y su sonido
habla también de la palabra que perdí)
— la que me buscaba dentro de una marea de
    lenguajes —
y hubiera probado con lo que tengo en la garganta hasta
    reventar,

I lost a word

> *I lost a word that was looking for me . . .*
> *a word in which I willingly lost you.*
> — P. Celan

the word with which one walks moves in advance
of the stride. and one already is that word,
a stroke ahead of what follows behind,
which is the body . . . a volume, a movement,
isolated from one's word, which opens up the path
    without losing the sense
of occupying the word's place. a fortification.
this morning the word woke me up
before moving my fingers, my eyelashes, the breeze, to
    suffocate
my egg and its luminosity; to satiate some of
its hunger to surge ahead as I fall behind,
not finding a body to support its majesty —
the squandering of syllables, replete from ethereal lips
pronouncing the roundness that outlines
and finally provokes that word. (because the cat has
sixteen word-mutilations and their sound
speaks too about the word I lost)
and with what I have in my throat,

con lo que tengo en la mente como prueba de Dios,
hasta calcinar su voz junto al sonido
y fundirlo en algo que te convenza.
allí, donde estás,
cómo te mueves sin una cuerda, sin una fibra,
que te sujete?

with what I have in my mind as proof of God,
the word would have tried until it burst,
until it charred its voice along with the sound
and fused them into something that might convince you.
there, where you are,
how do you move without a string, without a thread,
to hold you?

memoria o estatua

. . . *ha muerto un Dios cuyo culto consistía*
en ser besado . . .
— Pessoa (Antinoó)

la estatua de enfrente, a la distancia de mi mano, puede ser tocada suavemente. sus labios planos (único espacio de representación) realizan con mi gesto un vacío de palabras. no hay curiosidad, pero no puedo separar los dedos de esa boca de piedra caliza húmeda de alcohol, su sentido de la impasibilidad, de la inexpresividad es perfecto y me arrebata. la mano se detiene para que la estatua sea corrumpida y baje su cabeza en una sacudida del sentido y la bese. (una sangría) él besa mis dedos ligeramente — oh, dedos diestros! — y por la noche, mucho después, desde el siglo de la resurrección (Cristo — Antinoó) en el silencio del Gran Escultor, ruedan los bloques de marmól, se precipitan violentemente, caen a mis pies, a centímetros de civilizaciones ya desaparecidas y yo, acaricio con mi mano izquierda, el lugar donde puso sus labios esa estatua, tan imposible ahora, porque todo en ella es ornamento de otro ornamento, fiesta de la resurrección. el lugar donde se espera un cierto estreme–cimiento de la persona, no está en los tejidos, sino detrás de la nuca, en cada vértebra que se desliza como un teclado. repito la caricia en mi mente, allí puedo pasar toda la noche acariciándome. pero, para ser exacta, lo que más impresiona del gesto de un estatua es un prolongado uso

memory or statue

> . . . *a God has died whose worship consisted*
> *of being kissed . . .*
> — Pessoa ("Antinous")

the statue opposite, a hand's length away, can be touched
gently. its flat lips (sole space of representation) empty out
words with my gesture. there's no curiosity. but I can't take
my fingers away from that mouth, made of limestone and
wet with alcohol, its consciousness of impassivity, of
inexpressivity, is perfect and takes me away. my hand
pauses so the statue will rot, lower its head in a tremor of
sensation, kiss it. (a bloodletting) he kisses my fingers
gently — oh, skillful fingers! — and at night, much later,
from the century of resurrection (Christ — Antinous) in the
Great Sculptor's silence, the marble blocks roll, they plunge
violently down, they fall to my feet, inches from vanished
civilizations, and I, I caress with my left hand the place
where that statue put its lips, so impossible now, because
everything in it is an ornament of another ornament, a fes-
tival of the resurrection. the place where a little bodily
tremor is anticipated. it's not in the body's tissues, but at
the nape of the neck, in each vertebra that slips as if across
a keyboard. I repeat the caress in my mind, there, I can
spend all night caressing myself. but, to be exact, what is
striking about a statue's gesture is a prolonged use of

del deseo en la reiteración que se consume en pequeñas vibraciones o cláusulas al tacto, cuyos martinetes no rozan completamente atrás, no hay dolor, ya que no pretendan tocar o marcar un sonido. es sólo en ese sufrimiento de las fugacidad dentro del que uno espera la imagen de algún dios que parecía ser (su eco) que mis espasmos llegan con retraso, como el lento ensan–chamiento y la contracción del bigbang después de milenios, casi al amanecer. él amanece conmigo, dentro de mí, lo he robado de otros tiempos y ruinas — como una ola cuya alquimia arrastró con la resaca, lo podrido, lo muerto, lo brutal y que, con su pequeña llegada al amanecer, empieza a traer cosas vivas dentro de una humedad fría en exceso. no puedo alcanzarte todavía, no puedo llegar hasta ti . . . uno quiere robarle también a la estatua su seguridad, su intemporalidad, rendir la flaccidez que me ha humanizado y agoniza el ser de carne que soy, sus grietas, donde estuvo impuesta la carga del sentido inútil de padecer frente a ella. uno quisiera participar por dentro de la restauración, abrirse para hacer de nuevo un corazón junto al busto de Adriano, tras otra larga agonía . . . sobre el lecho profundo, por su desnudez total . . . pero los dioses han impuesto una niebla entre él y yo. entre él y su pasado — cuyo culto consistió en ser besado — y mi propia figura corrompida y echada contra el lecho entre tantas formas perdidas de la experiencia, o de lo real. él me recuerda el efecto generoso del desastre; un rostro sin arrugas que invita a la suposición ficticia de

desire, the repetition that dissolves itself into small vibrations or clauses when touched, whose piano-hammers don't touch down in the back; there's no pain, because they don't try to play or beat out a sound. it's only in that painful fleetingness, within which one awaits the image of some god who seemed to be (his echo), that my spasms arrive late, like the slow expansion and the contraction of the Big Bang after millennia, almost at dawn. he rises with me, within me, I've stolen him from other times and ruins — like a wave whose alchemy swept the rotten, the dead, the brutal away in its undertow and which, with its small arrival at dawn, brings living things in an excess of cold moisture. I still can't reach you, I can't get to you . . . one wants to steal the statue's security too, its intemporality, to surrender the flabbiness that has humanized me, and the fleshly being that I am agonizes; its cracks mark the heavy, useless awareness of suffering in front of the statue. inwardly one would like to participate in the restoration, to open up a heart and remake it next to the bust of Hadrian, after another long agony . . . "on the low bed, by his absolute nudity," but the gods have placed a fog between him and me. between him and his past — whose worship consisted of being kissed — and my own corrupt figure thrown onto the bed among so many lost shapes of experience, or of the real, he reminds me of the generous effect of disaster; unwrinkled face that invites the fictitious supposition

pasar dentro de la historia violándola con esta escena inmóvil y cruel de la inocencia. entonces tiemblo. tiemblo en mi recorrido estático fuera del arte. él no dice nada. la imagen de nuestro amor atravesará los siglos. reconstruiré una estatua más allá de una vida opresa en vida, opresa en sentido; escribiré de nuevo el poema "Antinoó" de Fernando Pessoa; escribiré de nuevo las memorias de Adriano, te besaré en los museos y despertarás de la cultura muerta en el espacio prolongado de la representación que es tu boca, sus labios planos, como un mapa del exceso de ti.

of entering history, violating it with this motionless and cruel scene of innocence. then I tremble. I tremble in my frozen path around the outside of art. he says nothing. the image of our love will span the centuries. I'll reconstruct a statue beyond a life oppressed in life, oppressed in consciousness; I'll write Fernando Pessoa's poem "Antinous" all over again; I'll write Hadrian's memories all over again, I'll kiss you in museums and you'll wake from the dead culture in the prolonged space of representation that is your mouth, its flat lips, like a map of the excess of you.

un momento de negrura

PARA MINNIE MARSH

siempre a las 10 de la mañana te encontraba cerca del parqueo. trucaba cientos de cosas antes de salir, cómo estaría mi rostro hoy, si había dormido bien, de qué hablaríamos, qué tiempo hace — no olvidar los espejuelos — cuánto dinero necesito, qué tal me va este color, cómo poner las venas dentro de las manos, absorber el refresco sin mancharme . . . a la distancia de mis ojos, otro rostro era siempre una censura, un bastión inexpugnable. a veces me contentaba tanto en las palabras que provenían del otro lado de la mesa, que sentía la formación de una nube mental (una burbuja) recreando las siluetas que formaban las imágenes de las imágenes, dentro de mis ojos. cuando ponía fin a este pequeño cine, me acordaba de ti y algunas veces de los otros. constantemente sentía el impulso obsesivo, abusivo — de abrazarte — de meter mi cabeza entre el desfiladero de la silla y la clavícula. allí descubría un pequeño lunar, una mancha de bronce, un lago para reposar y en el lago una flor, algo que estaría rozando después en el resto de las conversaciones estúpidas sin que los otros vieran, que mis ojos miraban hacia abajo, que acariciaban y sonreían al país de aquella mancha. claro, que saldría rápidamente del abrazo. qué haría yo con un abrazo así? enrojecer, mitificarlo, recordar . . . por las noches, la tensión de la energía recibida que me llevé (sin dar) no me dejaba dormir. como coágulos — dirías tú — se

a moment of blackness

FOR MINNIE MARSH

at 10 in the morning I would always find you near the parking lot. I would go over hundreds of things before leaving, how would my face be today, had I slept well, what would we talk about, what's the weather like — mustn't forget my glasses — how much money do I need, how well does this color suit me, how to make the veins in my hands disappear, how to drink my soda without getting it all over myself . . . from this distance, another face was always a censure, an unassailable fortress. at times I contented myself so much with words that originated from the other side of the table that I felt the formation of a mental cloud (a bubble), recreating silhouettes that images of images formed in my eyes. when I ended this little movie, I remembered you and sometimes the others. I constantly felt the obsessive, abusive impulse — to hold you — to fit my head into the space between the chair and your collarbone. there I discovered a small mole, a bronze stain, a lake for relaxation and in the lake a flower, something that I would later rub during the rest of the stupid conversations without the others noticing that my eyes looked downward, that they smiled at the country where that stain was and caressed it. of course, I would exit the embrace rapidly. what would I do with an embrace like that? blush, mythologize it, remember . . . at night, the tension of the received energy I took for myself (without giving) kept me from sleeping. like clots — you would say — they concen-

concentraban en mi interior dando punzadas bajitas, cabriolas en mis piernas y zumbidos de abejones en mis oídos. creo que he podido mirarte bien. creo que puedo recordar a la perfección, tu cuerpo y lo que está retenido en tu rostro. también creo, que hemos llegado al clímax, al broche de oro, de una red de metáforas y de hechos que concluyen en este deseo final. no sé por qué: te quiero abrazar . . . pero esa frase solemne, que reivindica toda mi vida es la frase con la que rezo a Dios siempre hacia el borde de la silla, con la pierna derecha cruzada sobre la izquierda (contra el tumor, el miedo, el ovario, la cruz) empujando a Dios, pidiéndole que me salve. pero cuál es mi Dios, cuál es el Dios de Minnie Marsh? llegábamos siempre en la bicicleta hasta el parqueo, donde la perra ámbar daba de mamar a sus perritos y entrábamos al hotel, decíamos "para dejar una crónica de su reconstrucción." el tragaluz, que tenía flores de colores me afectaba, no sabía qué lado de las sombras era más favorable a mi imaginación, a mi perfil. casi rígida, ella, Minnie Marsh, había llegado de Inglaterra, de la antigua Inglaterra de Virginia, de mi libro de relatos completos, con sus ojos gastados de ver tantos derrumbes, de abrir tanto el bolso y sacar la flor ajada y seca del vestido de terciopelo (de tu mancha) . . . yo también tengo mi flor! una flor es una recompensa que uno ha guardado contra los abusos de la superficie, contra los malos pensamientos de un "cualquier algo"; contra los límites de las rocas donde la visión podía deshacerse junto a las demarcaciones de la percepción,

trated themselves inside me, pricking me gently, skipping in my legs, and buzzing in my ears. I think I've been able to take a good look at you. I think I can remember, perfectly, your body and what your face retains. I also believe we've arrived at the climax, at the gold brooch, of a web of metaphors and of facts concluding in this final desire. I don't know why: I want to hold you. but that solemn sentence, which revindicates my whole life, is the sentence with which I pray to God, always on the very edge of my chair, with my right leg crossed over my left (against the tumor, the fear, the ovary, the cross), pushing God, asking him to save me. but who's my God, who's the God of Minnie Marsh? we always used to bike to the parking lot, where the amber bitch nursed her puppies and we entered the hotel, as we said, "to leave a chronicle of its reconstruction." the skylight, which had colored flowers, affected me, I didn't know which side of the shadows was more favorable to my imagination, to my profile. almost rigid, she, Minnie Marsh, had arrived from England, from Virginia's old England, from my book of complete tales, her eyes exhausted from seeing so many collapsed buildings. from opening her purse so often and taking the crumpled, dry flower out of the velvet dress (out of your stain) . . . I too have my flower! a flower is a reward that one has guarded against the abuses of the surface, against the bad thoughts of "whatever"; against the limits of rocks where vision can undo itself next to perception's demarcations, of the sign

139

del signo y de la imagen. una flor existía para mí, me demonstraba que esto ha sido, flota sobre la orilla del régimen atroz del amor. hace unos segundos que ella entró en tu cuerpo, en tu voz, en tu mente, en tu espíritu, tal como ella era en sí misma. está allí y es todas aquellas que en tu corteza de hombre puedas sostener desde una idea, o desde tu pene altísimo. quién dijo que era única? los rostros llevan las máscaras de lo que fueron, el guión y la censura de todos los rostros que participan siempre hasta el final; como los objetos llevan el alma, la pasión y hasta el descuido (el desenlace) en las protuberancias, de los símbolos que formaron, de los elementos que hallaron para su fusión. estamos aquí, otra vez en el proceso de la combustión, no sé por qué entraste en esta historia; no se por qué bajaste del tren que atravesaba los Alpes Suizos para estar aquí, junto a la iglesia gótica con sus rosetones que retienen hacia adentro amor y miedo, bajo los picos nevados del aire acondicionado del lobby de un hotel. no sé por qué, tu piel se hace más pálida cuando la miras, a medida que se aproxime, acerca y aproximan las doce campanadas y yo toco los cuadros de caballeros antiguos, yendo así de foto en foto, de jinete en jinete sin apocalipsis, de relieve en relieve para reconstruir la mano en su densidad, la mano en su profundidad, tal vez entre la tumba de algún faraón, o entre los restos de un naufragio que se ha consumido sin una imagen justa entre las algas. ahora, quizás, estás aquí, probablemente también reconstruyendo tus mentiras con las que formas tu pose votiva (que es

and of the image. a flower existed for me, it demonstrated to me that this has been, it floats above the edge of love's atrocious regime. a few seconds ago she entered your body, your voice, your mind, your spirit, such as she was in herself. she is there and she is all of them whom, in your manly exterior crust, you can support from an idea, or with your most erect penis. who said she was unique? the faces wear the masks of what they were, screenplay and censure of all the faces that always participate until the end; like the objects wear the soul, the passion and even the neglect (the outcome) in lumps of symbols that they formed, elements they found for their fusion. we are here, again in the process of combustion, I don't know why you entered this story; I don't know why you got off the train crossing the Swiss Alps to be here, next to the gothic church with its rose windows holding love and fear inside, beneath snowy peaks of air conditioning in the hotel lobby. I don't know why; your skin pales when you look at it, as you get closer, draw near, and the twelve peals of the bell come closer and I touch the portraits of ancient gentlemen, going like this from photo to photo, from horseman to horseman without apocalypse, from relief to relief to reconstruct the hand in its density, the hand in its depth, maybe, in some pharaoh's tomb, or among the remains of a shipwreck simply consumed without an image sharply marked on the seaweed. now, perhaps, you are here, probably also reconstructing your lies out of the ones that form your vo-

casi el compromiso de una vida) mientras yo te dibujo con la mano izquierda (tántrica) y toco tu ombligo debajo del pullover sudado y deshago todos los ovillos hechos por anteriores caricias, desde mi rincón de ser otra historia de Minnie Marsh (no era ella y sin embargo tampoco era otra persona) otra culpa de Minnie Marsh, que por descuido de su reloj infantil dejó caer a su hermano, a su queridísimo y único hermano de esta altura — porque yo estaba mirando un franja de tierra en la frase mientras él caía; o tal vez su padre se enamoró de "brillito de oro," como el la llamaba y no lo dejó quererla con sus celos de niña insuficiente, cuando lo ahogué en el río que arrastraba toda un vida (no la mía) sino de aquel a quien yo amaba en la oración. tal vez de obsesión de retener a todos estos hombres es no haberme entregado a ninguno — como Minnie Marsh sin rastro de sexo . . . qué se yo. cuando mueves la boca sé que estoy a esa inmensa distancia, de aquel fragmento de espacio y tiempo que es una vida. tendría que reconstruir escombro tras escombro, esas ruinas y volver a los parque, a los quicios, a las terminales con sus bancos húmedos donde me senté con una flor de ocho pétalos que es siempre virtualmente loca porque no mira nada presente y hace al mismo tiempo efecto de verdad, cuando retiene aquella mancha de bronce insignificante que es al fin su destino. pero es otra vez ese rostro de Minnie Marsh entrando en la historia, con sus botas abotonadas de nieve y la mancha de un gran acontecimiento que ocurrirá mientras miro tu nuca y ella no cesa de imitarme dentro de tus ojos — otra

tive pose (which is almost the commitment of a life) while I draw you with my left hand (tantric) and touch your bellybutton beneath your sweaty polo shirt and undo all the tangled lint made by previous caresses, from my angle as another Minnie Marsh story (it wasn't her and yet it wasn't anybody else), something else to blame on Minnie Marsh, that by a slip of a child's clock she let her brother fall, her dearest and only brother, from this height — because I was staring at a strip of the sentence while he fell; or maybe her father fell in love with "little ray of gold," as he called her, and didn't let him love her with the jealousy of an inadequate girl, when I drowned him in the river that dragged away a whole life (not mine) but that of the other person whom I loved in the prayer. maybe from obsessively retaining all those men comes not giving myself to any one — like Minnie Marsh without a trace of sex. what do I know. when you move your mouth I know I'm at an immense distance from that fragment of space and time which is a life. I would have to reconstruct debris piled on debris, those ruins, and I would have to return to the parks, to the doorjambs, to the terminals with their damp benches where I sat with an eight-petalled flower that's always almost crazed because it doesn't look at anything present and creates at the same time an effect of truth, when it retains that insignificant bronze stain that is finally its destiny. but again it's that face of Minnie Marsh entering the story, her boots buttoned up in the snow, with the stain of a great event that happened, while I look at the nape of your neck

vez champaigne — es ese acontecimiento, que por no ocurrir nos distorsiona los significados y se disuelve en un mal erótico y en una palidez que nos puede arrastrar a mí, a ella, tras el misterio de la simple concomitancia. tal vez hacia una ruina que no es de bronce, o de oro y quizás sea totalmente plástica y vulgar. en los momentos en que decaigo de este sentir pongo la proyección de la literatura y eso también cumple el sinuoso trayecto de mi línea. el temblor de una mano que se levanta para asegurar alguna cosa y se vuelve a posar (de esta forma no se me ven las venas) mi sangre se coagula sobre aquellas figuras de yeso, ha pasado por millones de años para aprender su inflexibilidad, ese juego de la luz a través del rosetón de lata por donde filtra el sol esta mañana lo que quiere. has encontrado a esta clase de mujer despiadada, que quiere ser cualquier mujer y todas las mujeres. no me dejes echarte en el cesto de las culpas, hay demasiada cultura en mi obsesión de velar por la belleza de su fealdad. Minnie, Minnie Marsh, con su rostro cubierto de polvos Mirurgia, su sombrerito con el ave del paraíso colgada pero sin volar desde la ventana. ah, ahí está también esa ventana — mirador que no tiene lugar y que no cesa de invitarme. yo siempre estaba en el alféizar, justo en el espacio de no ser paisaje, de no provocarme una inversión en el contorno de unos ojos . . . "los ojos de los demás son nuestras cárceles, sus pensamientos nuestras jaulas . . ." cómo hacer un lugar para no diluirme completamente en ti? me aferro al alféizar insinuando que nadie me permitió entrar o salir

and she still imitates me in your eyes — again champagne — it's that occurrence, which by not occurring distorts for us the meanings and dissolves into an erotic evil and a pallor that can drag us toward me, toward her, through the mystery of a simple concomitance. maybe toward a ruin that isn't bronze or gold and perhaps is thoroughly plastic, vulgar. while this feeling wanes in me, I project literature as a movie and that too completes my line's sinuous trajectory. the twitching of a hand that rises up to assure some thing and returns to rest (in this manner my veins can't be seen), my blood coagulates on those plaster figures, it has passed through millions of years to learn its inflexibility, that play of light through the tin rose window where the sun filters whatever it wants this morning. you've found this kind of ruthless woman, who wants to be any woman and all women. don't let me throw you into the basket with the blame, there's too much culture in my obsession of keeping watch for the beauty of her ugliness. Minnie, Minnie Marsh, her face covered with Mirurgia powder, her little hat with the bird of paradise hanging in but not flying from the window. ah, there is also that window— a bay window which has no place and still invites me. I was always on the windowsill, right in the space of not-landscape, of not-provoking in me an inversion contoured by eyes . . . "the eyes of others our prisons, their thoughts our cages . . ." how to create a place so I won't dilute myself completely in you? I cling to the sill, insinuating that nobody allowed me to enter or depart, and like that

y como esa mariposa — más bien un ave acuática del paraíso del sombrero de Minnie — no bajar, no mojarme. seguir así, columpiándome (ave por arriba, ave por abajo) en esta altura fingida por el miedo. mientras tanto, pensaba cómo sentir que quería abrazarte y no salir nunca de esta frase, buscando el sostén de esa columna vertical y gótica de esos huesos más fuertes de las letras; mientras mi boca se negaba a pronunciar algo, más fruncida, más apretada a la hilera de dientes de abajo, que se ven cada vez más con los años (uno empieza a morder desde abajo) y algo se ennegrecía allí, para hacer la larga noche de mi boca; me petrificaba como un oscuro yacimiento de saliva en mi postura señorial de Minnie Marsh, acercándose a un hombre alto y pálido que al abrazarla le acercaba un bastón para que no cayera aquel esqueleto de joven que quería entregarse todavía y para cuyo momento de negrura la piel ya no respondía y cerraba la boca, apretaba los labios, que antes fueron rosados y gruesos. (jamás podré escribir una novela. para escribir una novela necesitaría abrir esa ventana para que entraran bandadas de pájaros oscuros; tragar y engullirme las tóxicas opciones que tuve y no acepté. tendría que descruzar la pierna derecha de su cruz y decidir de qué lado del alféizar que hemos hecho, estar. seguir más allá del pliegue de la boca fruncida de su vestido gris de terciopelo y engullirme el pasado de otras bocas — como la tuya — dentro de tal oscuridad. tal vez, ya no sea posible devorar tanto tiempo acumulado.) cuál es el Dios de Minnie Marsh? el Dios de los callejones? el Dios de la

butterfly — rather, like an aquatic bird of paradise from Minnie's hat — to not-descend, to not-get-wet. to continue like this, swinging (bird above, bird below) at this height created by fear. meanwhile, I wondered how to feel that I wanted to hold you and never leave this sentence, seeking support for a vertical and gothic column of those stronger bones of words; while my mouth refused to pronounce anything, more wrinkled, more firmly pressed against the fine line of lower teeth, which are even more visible with the years (one begins to bite from below) and something was turning black there, to make my mouth's long night; it froze me like a dark deposit of saliva into my stately Minnie Marsh stance, approaching a tall, pale man, who upon embracing her gave her a cane so her youthful skeleton, which still wanted to give itself, wouldn't collapse, and to whose moment of blackness her skin no longer responded, and her mouth closed, her lips pursed, which before were pink and thick. (I'll never be able to write a novel. to write a novel I would need to open that window so that flocks of dark birds could enter; I would need to swallow and gulp the toxic options that I had and didn't accept. I would have to uncross my right leg from its cross and decide on which side of the sill that we've made I should be. continue beyond the fold, the frowning mouth of her gray velvet dress, and swallow the past whole out of other mouths — like yours — in such darkness. maybe it's no longer possible to devour so much accumulated time.) who's the God of Minnie Marsh? the God of the back streets? the God of old

vejez? el Dios de las tres de la tarde? yo también veo tejados, veo tu boca, que no me atrevo a tocar. pero, ay, no tengo ningún Dios en qué pensar, o cómo, de qué forma, con qué color imaginar que pienso en él. cuál será la frase final que fingiré decirle un segundo antes de morir . . . te quiero abrazar. y fue el aliento del refresco el que la petrificó y la convirtió otra vez en estatua de sal por haber pedido demasiado.

age? the God of three in the afternoon? I too see tiled roofs, I see your mouth, which I don't dare touch. but, oh, I don't have a single God to think about, or a way, in what form, with what color to imagine that I think about him. what will be the final sentence that I'll pretend to say to him one second before dying . . . I want to hold you. and it was the hint of soda that froze her and changed her back into a pillar of salt for having asked too much.

— al menos, así lo veía a contra luz —

PARA FERNANDO GARCÍA

he prendido sobre la foto una tachuela roja.
— sobre la foto famosa y legendaria —
el ectoplasma de lo que ha sido,
lo que se ve en el papel es tan seguro
como lo que se toca. la fotografía
tiene algo que ver con la resurrección.
— quizás ya estaba allí
en lo real en el pasado
con aquel que veo ahora en el retrato.
los bizantinos decían que la imagen de Cristo
en el sudario de Turín no estaba hecha
por la mano del hombre.
he deportado ese real hacia el pasado;
he prendido sobre la foto una tachuela roja.
a través de esa imagen (en la pared, en la foto)
somos otra vez contemporáneos.
la reserva del cuerpo en el aire de un rostro,
esa anímula, tal como él mismo,
aquel a quien veo ahora en el retrato
algo moral, algo frío.

era a finales de siglo y no había escapatoria.
la cúpula había caído, la utopía
de una bóveda inmensa sujeta a mi cabeza,
había caído.

— at least, that's how he looked, backlit —

FOR FERNANDO GARCÍA

I stuck a red tack into the photo
— into the famous, legendary photo —
the ectoplasm of what has been,
what you see on the paper is as secure
as what you touch. photography
has something to do with resurrection.
— maybe he was already here
in what was real, in the past
with the distant man whom I now see in the portrait.
the Byzantines said that Christ's image
on the shroud of Turin wasn't made
by the hand of man.
I've exiled that reality into the past;
I stuck a red tack into the photo.
through that image (on the wall, in the photo)
we're contemporaries again.
the body's reserve in a face's demeanor,
that speck of life, like the man himself,
that distant man whom I now see in the photo
something moral, something cold.

it was the end of a century and there was no way out.
the dome had fallen, the utopia,
an immense vault billowing from my head,
had fallen.

el Cristo negro de la Iglesia del Cristo
— al menos, así lo veía a contra luz —
reflejando su alma en pleno mediodía.
podía aún fotografiar al Cristo aquel;
tener esa resignación casual
para recuperar la fe.
también volver los ojos para mirar las hojas amarillas,
el fantasma de árbol del Parque Central,
su fuente seca.
(y tú que me exiges todavía alguna fe.)

mi amigo era el hijo supuesto o real.
traía los poemas en el bolsillo
del pantalón escolar.
siempre fue un muchacho poco común
al que no pude amar
porque tal vez, lo amé. la madre (su madre),
fue su amante (mental?)
y es a lo que más le temen.
qué importa si alguna vez se conocieron
en un plano más real.
en la casa frente al Malecón, tenía aquel
viejo libro de Neruda dedicado por él.
no conozco su letra, ni tampoco la certeza.
no sé si algo pueda volver a ser real.
su hijo era mi amigo,

the black Christ from the Church of Christ
— at least, that's how he looked, backlit —
reflecting his soul at high noon.
I could even photograph that distant Christ;
could have the casual resignation
to recover my faith.
could look again, too, at the yellow leaves,
at the ghost of a tree in Havana's Central Park,
its fountain dry.
(and you who still require faith from me.)

my friend was the supposed or real son.
he carried poems in the pocket
of his school uniform.
he was always an unusual boy,
one I couldn't love,
maybe because I loved him already. the mother (his
    mother)
was his (mental?) lover
and she is what they fear the most in him.
what does it matter if they once met each other
on a more real level.
in the house on the Malecón, he had that
old book by Neruda, dedicated.
I don't know what his handwriting was like — or
    certainty, either.
I don't know if anything can be real again.
his son was my friend,

entre la curva azul y amarilla del mar.
lo que se ve en el papel es tan seguro
como lo que se toca. (aprieto la tachuela roja,
el clic del disparador . . . lo que se ve no es la llama
de la pólvora, sino el minúsculo relámpago de una
foto).
el hijo (su hijo) vive en una casa amarilla
frente al Malecón — nadie lo sabe, él tampoco lo sabe —
es poeta y carpintero.
desde niño le ponían una boina
para que nadie le robara la ilusión de ser,
algún día, como él.
algo en la cuenca del ojo, cierta irritación;
algo en el silencio y en la voluntad
se le parece. entre la curva azul
y amarilla del mar.
— dicen que aparecieron en la llanura
y que no estaba hecha por la mano del hombre —
quizás ya estaba allí, esperándonos.
la verosimilitud de la existencia es lo que importa,
pura arqueología de la foto, de la razón.
(y tú que me exiges todavía alguna fe.)

el Cristo negro de la Isla del Cristo sigue intocable,
a pesar de la falsificación que han hecho
de su carne en la restauración;

between the blue and yellow curves of the sea.
what you see on the paper is as secure
as what you touch. (I press down on the red tack,
the click of the shutter . . . what you see isn't
the flash of gunpowder, but the tiny lightning
of a photo.)
the son (his son) lives in a yellow house
on the Malecón — no one knows it, he doesn't know it
    either —
he's a poet and a carpenter.
they've made him wear a beret since he was a child
so no one could steal his illusion that he would be,
someday, like his father.
something in the eye socket, a certain irritation;
something in the silence and in the resolve
seems like him. between the blue and yellow
curves of the sea.
— it's said they appeared on the plain
and the image wasn't made by the hand of man —
maybe he was already there, waiting for us.
the verisimilitude of existence is what matters,
the pure archeology of the photo, of reason.
(and you who still require faith from me.)

the black Christ from the Island of Christ is still
    untouchable,
in spite of the forgery they've made
of his flesh in the restoration;

la amante sigue intocable
y asiste a los homenajes en los aniversarios;
(su hijo) mi amigo, el poeta, el carpintero de Malecón,
pisa con sus sandalias cuarteadas
las calles de La Habana;
los bares donde venden un ron barato a granel
y vive en una casa amarilla
entre la curva azul y oscurecida del mar.
qué importancia tiene haber vivido
por más de quince años tan cerca del espiritú de aquel,
de su rasgo más puro, de su ilusión genética,
debajo de la sombra corrumpida
del árbol único del verano treinta años después?
si él ha muerto, si él también va a morir?

no me atrevo a poner la foto legendaria sobre la pared.
un simple clic del disparador, una tachuela roja
y los granos de plata que germinan
                    (su inmortalidad)
anuncian que la foto también ha sido atacada
por la luz; que la foto también morirá
por la humedad del mar, la duración;
el contacto, la devoción, la obsesión
fatal de repetir tantas veces que seríamos como él.
en fin, por el miedo a la resurrección,
porque a la resurrección toca también la muerte.

the lover is still untouchable
and attends homages on anniversaries;
(his son) my friend, the poet, the carpenter of the Malecón,
walks in cracked sandals through
the streets of Havana,
through bars where cheap rum overflows,
and lives in a yellow house
between the blue and darkened curves of the sea.
what does it matter to have lived
for more than fifteen years so close to the spirit of
that distant man,
to his purest feature, to his genetic illusion,
under the corrupted shadow
of the summer's only tree, thirty years later?
if he has died, if he too will die?

I don't dare put the legendary photo on the wall.
a simple click of the shutter, a red tack
and the germinating grains of silver
                         (his immortality)
announce that the photo has also been attacked
by the light; that the photo will also die
from the ocean's dampness, its duration;
the contact, the devotion, the fatal
obsession of repeating so many times that we would be
   like him.
anyway, I don't dare for fear of resurrection,
because resurrection too is touched by death.

sólo me queda saber que se fue, que se es
la amante imaginario de un hombre imaginario
                    (laberíntico)
la amiga real del poeta de Malecón,
con el deseo insuficiente del ojo que captó
su muerte literal, fotografiando cosas
para ahuyentarlas del espíritu después;
al encontrarse allí, en lo real en el pasado
en lo que ha sido
por haber sido hecha para ser como él;
en la muerte real de un pasado imaginario
— en la muerte imaginaria de un pasado real —
donde no existe esta fábula, ni la importancia
o la impotencia de esta fábula,
sin el derecho a develarla
(un poema nos da el derecho a ser ilegítimos en algo
    más
que su trascendencia y su corruptibilidad).
un simple clic del disparador
y la historia regresa como una protesta de amor
                    (Michelet)
pero vacía y seca. como la fuente del Parque Central
o el fantasma de hojas caídas que fuera su árbol
    protector.
ha sido atrapada por la luz (la historia, la verdad)
la que fue o quiso ser como él,
la amistad del que será no será jamás su hijo,

the only thing that's left for me is to know that I was,
   that I am
the imaginary lover of an imaginary man
                    (labyrinthine)
the real friend of the poet of the Malecón,
with the same insufficient desire as the eye that captured
his literal death, photographing things
in order to drive them away from the spirit afterwards;
finding myself there, in what is real, in the past,
in what has been,
by having been made in order to be like him;
in the real death of an imaginary past
— in the imaginary death of a real past —
where this fable doesn't exist, or the importance
or the impotence of this fable,
without the right to unveil it
(a poem gives us the right to be illegitimate in something
more than its transcendence and its corruptibility).
a simple click of the shutter
and history returns like a declaration of love
                 (Michelet)
but empty and dry. like the fountain in Central Park
or the ghost of fallen leaves that was once its protective
   tree.
she has been trapped by light (history, truth)
the woman who was or who wanted to be like him,
the friendship with the one who will be, who will never
   be his son,

la mujer que lo amó desde su casa abierta,
anónima, en la página cerrada de Malecón;
debajo de la sombra del clic del disparador
abierto muchas veces
en los ojos insistentes del muchacho
cuya almendra oscurecida
aprendió a mirar
y a callar
como elegido.
(y tú me exiges todavía alguna fe?)

the woman who loved him from her open house,
anonymous, on the closed page of the Malecón;
under the shadow of the shutter's click
opened many times
in the boy's insistent eyes,
darkened almonds that
learned to see
and to be silent
as if chosen.
(and you still require some faith from me?)

Afterword:
The Only Moment I Will Witness

BY KRISTIN DYKSTRA

Reina María Rodríguez was born in Havana in 1952, less than a decade before the Cuban Revolution took place. The revolution shaped the world in which she grew up: her education, her career as a writer, the institutions that have supported artistic dialogue and exchange central to her experience, the books available for her to read. By emphasizing the importance of this context, however, I do not wish to suggest that Rodríguez' writing can be reduced to political statement, or that its value lies only in holding up a mirror to institutional structures in her nation. In her most evocative imagery, Rodríguez saturates intimate experience with meditations on revolution, history, and aesthetics.

"What matters," Rodríguez states, is an approach to writing that she associates with John Cage:

> Incorporating everything. In other words, not differentiating between literature and the life I'm living. I think that conserving it there as the work . . . It's like capital accumulated toward our possibility of really achieving a powerful state. Not greater, but broader, a passion or a form. Because in each of my books, what has always mattered is the human form of existence itself. Existing and seeing what is happening.[1]

Incorporating "everything" allows Rodríguez to conceive of her work as poetic testimony, linking everyday personal

experience to public dialogues about community and history.

Delving into the contents of Rodríguez' testimonials requires early acknowledgment of a geographical fact: she continues to live in the city of Havana. Because many other writers and artists have left the island in past decades, critic Catherine Davies reminds us, "In Cuba, staying home is a conscious, political decision" (2). What, then, does it mean to stay *and* to speak through poetry? To craft a life as an intellectual in a revolutionary society?

For Rodríguez, it means approaching these questions with great care. While her life on the island clearly provides both intimate and historical imagery for her poems, she consistently resists heavy-handed polemics. She uses poetry to create delicate disruptions in the fabrics of personal and social experience. In "the islands," for example, she destabilizes certainties by imagining "an interval between two kinds of time" and naming the island a "tenuous place." Her depiction of island time and space — here, as solitude adrift between ebb and flow — contributes to dialogues about the meaning of "insularity," a repeating issue in Cuba's literary history. Rodríguez joins a longer conversation about envisioning community — both lived and utopian — with critical and intellectual awareness.

Describing Rodríguez' contributions to this dialogue can be tricky, not only because of her use of ambiguous and shifting images, but also because of debates about what it means to have a critical vision in her context. Desiderio Navarro argues that the intellectual occupied a shifting

position in late twentieth-century Cuban society, based on divided ways of perceiving the value of "critical" questions. One reader, presuming that critical engagement pays the highest compliment to revolutionary society, might see in Rodríguez' poetry an unflagging commitment to an idealized revolutionary freedom and its literature. Another reader could presume the opposite: that her combination of critical vision and literary cosmopolitanism produces negative representations of an island doomed always to fall short of utopia, leaving the poet in the role of the vocal outcast.

Pushed to its extreme, either view would probably be inaccurate for describing Rodríguez' poems. The poems negotiate commitments made possible *between* polarities of hope and despair. They open windows into multiple levels of daily life in Havana. These poems describe relationships — among people, objects, ideas, different parts of the self. How coherent, Rodríguez asks us, is personal identity? How do we negotiate demands made on us by others, be they our fellow members of society or the ghostly alternative selves residing in the back of one's head? What allows us to become aware of our own imbrication in social experience, recognizing elements of our identities which remain incomplete or unavailable until they are activated by others?

Rodríguez approaches many of these recurring themes through scenes of desire. Desire tends to be sexual in her poems, and it is also visionary in a broader social sense, opening the self/"I" to shifting relations with others.

Exploring connection, her poems draw on the fundamental presumption that words *are* relations, in and of themselves. Language that may initially appear private, even self-absorbed, can contain embedded relationships with others, avoiding forms of isolation in which "the self is rendered senseless."[2] As a foundation for her poetics, the need for relation with others has long been accompanied — and symbolized — by Rodríguez' determined participation in literary dialogues and organizations, some formal and others informal.

Here, I share Rodríguez' own remarks about her life and work as a writer, placing her testimony next to some commonly recognized landmarks of Cuban public and literary life. Interviews with the poet span several important historical moments, provisionally linked by her experience: the end of the Cold War, the "Special Period" of the 1990s, and a disorienting new millennium. As I write this Afterword, Cuba's revolutionary intervention in world history appears to have split the island into many different "apparent worlds"[3]: a proud and hopeful survivor of time and conflict; a national body and soul pervaded by corruption; an expired revolutionary dream (worn-out clothing held up only by Castro's aged frame); and a resistance reborn, one ever seeking creative ways to envision the future. Visions of utopia move with the ebbs and flows that make up the living surface of history, like the "motions and contortions of the sea."[4]

The Making of the Writer

When very young, still unable to read, Rodríguez carried books of poetry around her house and pretended to understand their contents. At school she began to write poems. "But my true destiny," she remembers, amused, "was to be a dancer: I studied dance (and piano) for many years. Later, an illness forced me to spend a prolonged period resting, so I became a dedicated reader: Salgari, Dumas, Verne. At 13 I read *A Portrait of the Artist as a Young Man* and, in a rather vague way, I perceived that it was a different book than those that I habitually read. And one fine day I began to read Martí,[5] some of whose pages I learned from memory by turning them so often."[6] Rodríguez somewhat casually reveals that unusual literary resources were available to her during her enforced bed rest: "Below my house was the National Press, and at that time Alejo Carpentier[7] was the director. His secretary was a great friend of mine, and she brought me boxes of books. In other words, that was my literary 'context,' dating from when I was twelve or thirteen years old."[8] In these memories, we see the doubled ground underneath her writing: an early exposure to European modernism; and the canonical, yet local, influences of Cuban writers Martí and Carpentier.

Rodríguez went on to study art history, later switching to Pan-American literature at the University of Havana, where she won her first poetry prize. After college she worked in Cuban radio, television, and the publications *La Gaceta de Cuba* and *Prensa Latina*. She participated in writers' workshops. Rodríguez also began work with the Saíz

Brothers' Brigade, an organization active on both provincial and national levels. Participating in the Brigade for approximately ten years gave her the opportunity to travel around the island, meeting artists and writers as she organized cultural events. One memorable visit took her to the Matahambre Mines in Pinar del Río, where she read her poetry and presented a new book underground — literally (in one of the mines).

Eventually, however, Rodríguez decided that she had to commit less time to organizational activities and more time to her own growth as a writer. This growth would take place within a cultural climate that could be both encouraging and tense. Literary production in contemporary Cuba is supported to a much greater extent than it was prior to the Revolution, when literacy rates were low and there was little financial backing for local publishing projects. Writers often had to pay to publish their own work and took it for granted that the best career opportunities existed with foreign publishers, who were not necessarily inclined to support emerging writers. In the sixties, the revolutionary government's literacy campaign rapidly created a brand-new Cuban reading public, an audience which could appreciate work steeped in local concerns and traditions.[9] The Cuban government encouraged and promoted the arts with publishing opportunities and other forms of support, such as the creation of numerous state-sponsored *talleres*, or workshops. Governmental writers' unions helped to sponsor a boom in writing production and publication. An institution which has drawn interest worldwide is Casa de

las Américas, the publishing house founded on the island by Haydee Santamaría after the revolution. Casa de las Américas was seen by many as an important step in the promotion of Havana as "an alternative capital of the Americas," providing the "possibility of some sense of a new, pan-American postcolonial identity."[10] Literary prizes offered by the publishing house continue to carry tremendous prestige. To date, Rodríguez has won two Casa de las Américas prizes for poetry, which continue to inspire interest in her work worldwide.

The downside of the revolutionary government's construction of a new and local culture came with the difficulty of housing artistic and intellectual work within institutions overseen by the state. Censorship resulted in two forms: overt governmental actions and individual self-silencing. Seeking to clarify the state's position on cultural work, Fidel Castro delivered the "Palabras a los intelectuales" speech ("Words for the Intellectuals") in 1961. This proclamation outlined the role of the artist in the revolutionary society, best summarized in Castro's famous phrase, "Dentro de la Revolución, todo; contra la Revolución, nada" ("Everything within the Revolution, nothing against the Revolution"). Navarro observes that this phrase lent ambiguity rather than clarity: it "proved to be extraordinarily polysemic, which allowed it to become the guiding principle for the successive periods and tendencies in struggle" (188). The same proclamation could support or suppress expression:

> The country's cultural and social life would re-
> peatedly bring up . . . questions that never got a
> well-developed, clear, and categorical answer:
> Which events and processes of Cuban social and
> cultural reality form part of the Revolution and
> which do not? How can one distinguish which
> cultural texts or practices act against the Revo-
> lution? Which act for it? And which simply do
> not affect it? Which social criticism is revolution-
> ary and which is counterrevolutionary? Who de-
> cides what is the correct answer to these
> questions? How and according to what criteria
> is this decision made? Does *not* going against the
> Revolution imply silence on the social ills of the
> prerevolutionary past that have survived or on
> the ills that have arisen due to erroneous politi-
> cal decisions and unresolved problems of the
> revolutionary period? Doesn't being for the Revo-
> lution imply publicly revealing, criticizing, and
> fighting these social ills and errors? And so on.
> (Navarro 188)

The contradiction between the Revolution's strong support of artistic production and its potential desire to control the artist's message bureaucratically was dramatically illustrated by the "Padilla affair." In 1968, a young poet named Heberto Padilla wrote a book of poetry entitled *Fuera del juego*. Nominated for a prestigious national literary prize, his book seemed sure to win — but its content was deemed

counterrevolutionary by several members of the UNEAC (National Union of Cuban Writers and Artists), as was that of Padilla's counterpart in the category of drama, Antón Arrufat. *Fuera del juego* and Arrufat's play ultimately won in their respective fields. The prize was publication by UNEAC. However, the union inserted prologues declaring that "this poetry and this theater serve our enemies, and their authors are the artists that our enemies need to fatten the Trojan horse until the time when imperialism decides to put its politics of direct aggression against Cuba into practice."[11]

The Padilla affair did not end with the publication of *Fuera del juego*. In 1971 Padilla was arrested and charged with conspiring against the Revolution. After his release, on the night of April 17, 1971, Padilla delivered a "self-criticism," an exaggerated proclamation of guilt. Padilla's performance of denouncing his previous activities and counterrevolutionary behavior took place before an audience of party officials and fellow UNEAC members. The "self-criticism" spoke volumes about links between dissent and discourses of guilt in island culture. Meanwhile, it had far-reaching repercussions, serving to polarize the Latin American intellectual community as to the role of politics in artistic production, and variations on this debate continued for the rest of the century.[12] Such was the backdrop for Cuba's successive generations of writers and artists, who would experience variable degrees of openness and restriction in the official cultural policies of the decades to follow.[13]

Cuban culture, then, is buffeted by competing and para-

doxical energies of experiment and containment. Perhaps they are inevitable within the oxymoronic yet living condition of the "revolutionary state." The fact that Rodríguez, like Padilla and others, frequently writes about guilt in multivalent forms suggests that life among these competing forces is neither guilt-free nor easily judged.

Conversationalism and Beyond: Developing "The Poetic"

Rodríguez published her first collection of poems, *La gente de mi barrio* (*The People of my Neighborhood*), in 1976. Today she describes the collection as her most conversational writing: it is poetry spoken through everyday language and based on local concerns. Rodríguez received the March 13 Prize from the University of Havana for this first book, and her poems were reprinted in Cuban periodicals.

At the time, conversationalist poetics were influential both for Latin America in general and revolutionary Cuba in particular. Even as she worked within conversationalism, though, Rodríguez had begun to look for a different approach to poetry. She recalls, "I always wanted to provoke 'the poetic'; that is, I was always looking for the metaphor. That's why there were many assonances and terms that I've since discarded."[14] Four years later, Rodríguez published *Cuando una mujer no duerme* (*When a Woman Can't Sleep*).[15] She remembers tension that continued to develop in the process of this writing: "I experienced a conflict between something that was 'the poetic' for me, 'the sym-

bolic,' and something else that was the colloquial language of the street, something direct. The result was a blend of the two" (IDGM). *Cuando una mujer no duerme* won the 1980 UNEAC Honorable Mention for poetry. Still, something was missing. Rodríguez selected the poem "debts" for this anthology, noting that it represents her work of this period well. However, she now observes that she can no longer write in this mode: "It's very sincere; I realize that for me, it acts as a formula for writing. Everyone was asking me for 'debts.' Anywhere I went to read, people asked me for it and copied it down. I thought that writing in this way could achieve terrific communication. But a moment came when it was very easy, and I was going to repeat this structure whose greatest virtue was its sincerity. I decided that I had to break completely with this model." [16]

In her third book, *Para un cordero blanco* (*For a White Lamb*, 1984), Rodríguez continued to wrestle with the balance between the major elements of her poetic voice. She prioritized the symbolic aspect of language, something that could go beyond "themes that grew out of my daily life, out of my world of little things" (IDGM), although those everyday elements continued to bring intimacy to her work. In search of "the poetic," she read avidly, telling the magazine *Cuba Internacional* about her interest in José Martí, César Vallejo, Nazim Hikmet, Roque Dalton and Jaime Sabines. She also read widely in biographies, newspapers, compilations of letters, and essays. Like many of her contemporaries, she acknowledged the strong influence of Soviet film on her work (and would return to this interest in

visual languages in a later project inspired by photography).

Para un cordero blanco was awarded the 1984 Casa de las Americas prize for poetry. Rodríguez says, "People bought the book. My name became known. But I wanted to look for other routes. It was important to push myself further toward something that, for me, is what it means to be a writer. And that was much more than just shouting, speaking out, or saying that I had this or that problem. I spent eight years really reading a lot. Philosophy and religion interested me — all those stories created in religion — and I wrote two books" (IDGM). The first of these two books was *En la arena de Padua* (*On the Sands of Padua*). Rodríguez describes the sense of guilt she felt as she began to write *Padua*, still torn between the populist influences of conversationalism and the more philosophical, symbolic tone that she was trying to develop.

Between 1988 and 1990, Rodríguez participated in Paideia, a critical intervention in the island's cultural scene. The interdisciplinary movement sought to put cultural programming under the control of artists and writers themselves, rather than in the hands of bureaucrats and institutions. Paideia captured the alternative spirit of the decade, pushing at the boundaries of institutional culture: "An extraordinary proliferation of cultural spaces of all kinds took place during the 1980s: spaces for exhibits, publication, readings, discussions; institutional and noninstitutional spaces; private and public spaces" (Navarro 192). Rodríguez remembers Paideia as "a romantic idea. Very Gramscian — the idea of the organic intellectual."[17] She

fondly recalls the strong feelings of unity that writers experienced with actors, visual artists, and musicians at crowded events.

However, Paideia did not lead to a new or utopian era for writers and artists — instead, many of them, particularly visual artists, soon left the island. By 1988, Navarro writes, "The intellectual's critical intervention in the public sphere was opposed by a new offensive that — in conjunction with the difficult working and living conditions created by the economic crisis of the early 1990s, and the simultaneous loosening in the granting of exit permits — led the majority of that artistic intelligentsia to join the diaspora in the Americas and in Europe" (192-3). In Rodríguez' opinion, cultural institutions retook the "organic intellectual" and constructed versions of that creature to fit their own image. Paideia participants went off in their own directions, some remaining on the island and others moving into varieties of exile.

While bureaucratic interference motivated some exiles, the economic crisis to which Navarro refers was significant and soon became one of the most broadly shared experiences of the 1990s: the "Special Period." Developments in international politics had set the stage for this crisis. With the fall of the Soviet Union near the end of the '80s, Cuba's main sources of economic aid disappeared along with trading partners. Furthermore, the nation suffered a loss in prestige, one based on military collaborations abroad: "Whether as a result of battlefield victories that no longer required a Cuban military presence or at the request

of governments and as a result of international negotiations, the return of Cuban troops to their homeland in the early 1990s put an end to a remarkable chapter in Cuba's international relations and markedly reduced Cuba's influence in the world beyond its boundaries."[18] The U.S. trade embargo — called "the blockade" by Cubans — now affected the populace more deeply than ever.

Citizens could no longer rely on the state to provide food and other basic necessities, and the result was the rise of a thriving informal economy. The black market came to be intimately connected to the tourist economy of the island, where pockets of capitalism provided opportunities for the everyday citizen trying to cope with the shortages. While the average Cuban was paid in pesos and expected to operate in the peso economy, U.S. dollars ironically drove the businesses of the more lucrative tourist sector in spite of the embargo. As a result of this dual economic system, many Cubans sought ways to earn dollars through activities such as the operation of illegal taxis, the sale of Cuban cigars, or prostitution. Others relied on help from relatives outside the island to cope with the scarcities. Aging buildings in the city of Havana, not receiving long-awaited repairs, began to show the physical strains aggravated by the economic crisis. The state encouraged foreign investment in new tourist hotels and sponsored renovation projects to convert parts of the colonial sector of town into tourist attractions, but other buildings in the city collapsed. For many citizens, "home" included crumbling balconies, broken windows, and ghostly lots where buildings once had stood.

Rodríguez composed *Padua* in the late '80s, coinciding with the Paideia years and the beginning of the new and difficult experience of everyday life in the Special Period. The poems reflect the disillusion and daily hardships faced by citizens struggling to make ends meet. They also reflect the need to respond creatively to crisis.

A striking aspect of the poetry from *Padua* is the appearance (and disappearance) of ruins, structures, and other architectural images. These lend emotional richness and also serve as metaphors for the human body and mind. "The rafters," in which the speaker asserts, "My life is tilted," reveals the inadequacy of structures both literal and figurative, evoking the loss of stability in the Special Period. From one poem to the next in *Padua*, the speaker seems isolated, even suspended in silence, perhaps talking only to herself or to an absent listener, a "holographic memory."[19] The speaker documents her own disappearance from "a deserted beach and an empty house."[20] Considering this book in retrospect, Rodríguez recalls "the pain that you feel when you don't want to have hope anymore after having believed in a utopia . . . when what you've expected has always been frustrated." In individual poems she now sees a kind of pain created by intense political pressures on writers: "the trace of ideological oversaturation, of the frustration that utopia left behind in me. It works on a very personal plane, on a level of language" (IDGM).

Padua reflects the need to question language as structure: many poems comment on the generation of narra-

tives through which we perceive the world. In "Poliedros/polyhedrons," self becomes "simulacrum," a repeating shape, a copy. The poem dramatizes the splitting of identity into separate fields or elements: body, narrative, ritual, and a partially articulated consciousness reminiscent of the ephemeral writer in Jorge Luis Borges' short story of self-loss, "Borges and I." If Rodríguez describes a fractured self in "polyhedrons," the community gaze exacerbates the problem rather than resolving it. Family members are no more helpful than anyone else in finding the speaker's most authentic and familiar self. Instead, the speaker claims a location in strangeness — that is, inside a domestic and bodily strangeness, in "the strange womb of a woman who copies a common sort of existence and lays out a tablecloth fabricated from illusion, but who also hopes for an alternative life."[21]

"Paradise. Storefront. Monte street," also from *Padua*, depicts a wave of nausea Rodríguez felt while passing a house full of objects that had been seized by the government:

> The ventilator
> blades are tired   of lifting dust over
> these lifeless objects.
> objects in disuse. exhaling. restlessness.
> on a sinuous street an abandoned store
> and it's June it's called paradise.
> pressed against the window I'm chewing straw
> and see nothing specific definable: nothing
>   costly

the point being not to die not to see
a boredom that once pertained to light
stains here and there
no one knows what of.
spent   timeworn   nothing costly
waiting for a buyer to come: useless garment
my left breast out from under my blouse
there's a whetstone.
the rats watch us, distrust us, watch us
their reddish eyes behind a cardboard box.
items that meant something once
simulation. ovation.
the melody is mediocre   a music blending
          droning
to complaints from the fan
blades shuddering against themselves.
   something moves
seems to move.
old lamps old artifice: nothing costly
mirrors only images
the opaque mercury against the eye of a
    previous object.
we are sick of the performance and the
    indemnity.
the street sinuous: storefront. monte street.
    paradise.
setting down the second-hand store that
    allured me
ok I was looking

but now nothing's antique not even
the proximity of their forms to curb the illusion
among so many objects of no use no destiny
resigned to their silent routine
when not
otherwise piled together [22]
      — Translated by Roberto Tejada

After completing the poem, Rodríguez realized that it was "very strong, in a critical and social sense" (IDGM): in "Paradise. Storefront. Monte Street," paradise is a jumble of outworn forms, objects with no "use" or "destiny." By stating, "we are sick of the performance and the indemnity," the speaker establishes an important similarity between herself and her community. She is not isolated but representative in her frustration. How, then, might paradise be reformulated? If one gives utopia a new shape, can it move beyond artifice or simulacrum to reality? Such questions would continue to underlie later projects.

While *Padua* contained some of the most socially critical texts in Rodríguez's career, the poet adds that the experience of writing the collection also helped her to arrive at a satisfying balance between aesthetic forces that had previously seemed to clash in her writing. The book's voice is "not in one language or in the other, but it's somewhere else, like what I had been trying to achieve" (IDGM). Rodríguez does not specify where this point of arrival is, and her evasion is not coincidental. Evasion gives her freedom in difference. By describing her "artifice" only as be-

ing *somewhere else*, she avoids constructing a narrative that would arrive neatly at a specified destination on pre-laid tracks. The final lines of "polyhedrons" reflect — and reflect on — the paradoxical creation of closure via an act of displacement: "as if there were always an after, an elegant ending to invent the things that happened and that didn't happen — metaphor that gets lost on the river's opposite bank — and maybe those things will happen?"

Moving "somewhere else" within poetic language, toward questions rather than answers, also meant rethinking her interests in poetry as a genre. During the composition of *Páramos (Plains)*, Rodríguez worked somewhere between prose and poetry. "I don't see a clear division between poetry and prose," she states. "But I don't think I consider this writing to be 'prose poetry,' either. . . . It's characterized by a more free verse, a verse that can include moments of rhyme, that takes you to another level of structure itself" (IDGM). She explains that her interest in language had developed: "Words are acquired from many places, to play their roles, wherever I put them. Language does interest me, not historical acts but language, the movement and actions that occur in language itself" (IDGM).

Memory results from these movements and actions in *Páramos*. However, Rodríguez specifies that memory can be experienced in nonlinear form. The entire book feels to her "as if an artist cut her head open and the entire social experiment and all of this daily life were carried inside, to a purely interior plane, where there are different points of

motion. They move on different levels of consciousness" (IDGM). Philosophical readings helped her to pursue her versions of social experimentation:

> I was reading Marshall Berman's book, *All That Is Solid Melts into Air*. It's a book about the city, about how a city becomes a postmodern city, and why . . . I also read Baudrillard. I read a lot of Lyotard. I read Foucault. But fundamentally, beyond the individual texts — of which there may be nothing left — I think the constant interest for me in all the books I've written has centered on the idea of being something reproduced within the space of underdevelopment, in pseudo-socialism, in kitsch, in a tropical region. In other words, how do you inject any world or place with what Jorge Zalamea has said — that there are no pueblos, and there are no underdeveloped peoples? (DSDE)

As she constructed *Páramos*, the writing felt risky. The collection was densely written, highly complex. Its complexity, however, had an emotional base. Rodríguez felt a strong need to write in engagement with her intellectual community:

> We had this terrible complex . . . We felt that ideology was supplanting thought. That's a real conflict. More than being from my generation, I think it's from the next one, the one that continued after us. There was a rhetoric — a rehashing of thought

from the French or German world — and with very little grounding, really, in Cuban literature itself and in Cuban thought of the nineteenth century. In other words, it was grafted onto the culture. This isn't bad, for me; I think we had very few other options at the time. And that thought was a very interesting option. It passed quickly, but in my case, more than anything else, it left me *Páramos*, marked with the traces of those authors. Above all, with postmodern thought. (DSDE)

Rodríguez worried that *Páramos* would find no readership. But the book quickly sold out.

As Rodríguez noted, language contained internalized versions of the revolutionary social experiment. "Violet Island" is a socially critical poem that refers to a story about a lighthouse-keeper. He falls asleep on the job. Rodríguez explains, "Because he falls asleep, ships are wrecked. The result is a disaster. The woman [in 'Violet Island'], just like that lighthouse-keeper, wants to experience spiritual enlightenment; she wants to understand many things; but she falls asleep, she stays asleep, and she loses that possibility. So the social situation is depicted through the relationship between the woman and the lighthouse-keeper at Aspinwall."[23] Throughout the poem, the speaker links abstracted social commentary to reflections on poetry and form: can this writing be used to tell a community story while also serving as a space for withdrawal from narra-

tive languages? The dilemma pits two of the speaker's desires against each other. First, she claims, "I wanted life only for the pleasure of dying on the quiet waters." However, self-loss is not sufficient, even if tinged with personal spirituality: she moves on to say, "Maybe they can understand my intention / to still tell the story of some shadow, some light." The final section of the poem, beginning "and now tell me," attempts to tell this story in compact lines. We hear the story of an urban past: "it was a city with a port. / the names of its deep ships / once anchored here." The telling of this communal (hi)story, as in other Rodríguez poems, ends in questions: "where is the port? / and the ships? / and the lighthouse? / and the shoulders of the sailors inviting you / to other dark ports?"

Another poem, "luz acuosa / watery light," has similarly drawn attention for literary experimentation and social critique. It uses sexuality and pain in both intimate and public ways, perhaps best approached through performance artist Magaly Muguercia's observation, "There are rhythms, tensions, attacks, and convolutions — vibrations of the body that make history" (182). Rodríguez, who suffers from a painful medical condition that she mentions in the poem, makes the links between body, city, and history in "watery light" explicit: "The city is like a uterus that is bleeding; all of my friends leaving when we were in our twenties, and again when we turned forty, and more are leaving now" (IDGM).

"Watery light" has a distinct moment of origin in her mind: "I had a fever and was lying on a cushion and my house

was deteriorating — there have been repairs, and more repairs," she recalls. "There I was, when suddenly there was a strong gust of wind. A friend of mine, whom I love very much, left to go back to New York" (IDGM). This problem of vanishing friends not only appears in the poem but affected its composition: Rodríguez notes that she was trying to write *Páramos* among a circle of fellow island intellectuals, adding that "people around me are always a point of reference, like places of arrival, like mirrors" (DSDE). What happens when instead those people are departing, bodies disappearing, leaving only one's own reflection in the mirror?

Throughout "watery light," Rodríguez blends pain with wry humor and rich coloration. Sex is depicted through the voice of a woman who is semi-alienated from her body, yet the poem allows for moments of pleasure and suggests a possible communion (if sacrificial) with or after climax. The "bleeding uterus" represents losses — of blood, but also of people — which are not healthy or natural (as compared to, say, normal rhythms of menstruation). This unhealthy loss hints that the poem's eroticism, its openness to the outside, may also be threatening, despite the dry humor that recurs throughout the poem. Rodríguez highlights this threat by hinting at complicity, saying that the Havana of "watery light" is, in part, "a city that wants to be violated" (IDGM). Again, Muguercia is helpful: Cuban culture of the 1990s

> engendered a 'loose' body, not only in the sense
> of freed or untied but also in the sense of "es-

caped," thrown out of gear, in some way autonomous or alone. This is how, at a certain level of analysis, formations such as the self-seeking or prostituted body, the body of illegality and "hustling" (*bisneo*), and also of anomie, appear to me. The body of exile. The loose body generates multiple scenarios, from the picaresque to self-exile to madness and suicide. (184)

Here, "looseness" corresponds in part to common English-language connotations (ex. the female body that is sexually out of control, even prostituted), but it also connotes an enriched set of ideas: a general state of unsettled and/or unnatural relations in social history. It is the body's vibration to a harsh and "special" period of crisis. The loose body's greatest power and importance may come from its contrast to a "genuine moral body," one of the central and stabilizing icons of Cuban nationalist discourse since the early nineteenth century.[24]

In *La foto del invernadero* (*The Photo of the Greenhouse*), a collection of poetry published in 1998, Rodríguez combined the transgressive writing of *Páramos* with a return to more traditional forms. Time is the central theme of these meditations. The back-narrative of the collection is about a woman flipping through the UNESCO *Courier*, looking at photographs of other places and times. As we read the finished poems, we "look through the photos of places and people as if everything has frozen, turned to ice" (IDGM).

The woman flipping through the pages is someone not

quite Rodríguez herself but a fictional döppelganger mimicking her motions. "I was trying to really desacralize something, using 'her,'" Rodríguez says. "'She' is the device that I currently use to resolve issues between the 'you' and the 'I' — 'she is a writer who turns the pages of a magazine, trying to pull the past out of its depths, trying to find it. The past is lost in the photographs" (DSDE). Rodríguez sees the book as documentation of "a time of great exhaustion, in which all landscapes are submerged" (DSDE).

As in *Páramos*, imagery of the body anchors many poems in *Foto*. They emerge from history: Rodríguez describes "time turning into statues which, in some way, at some time, have belonged to me." The poem "a moment of blackness," based on a short story by Virginia Woolf, uses the character of Minnie Marsh. Changes in her aging body support a metanarrative about the pending collapse of emotional and linguistic structures: "I wondered how to feel that I wanted to hold you and never leave this sentence, seeking support for a vertical and gothic column of those stronger bones of words; while my mouth refused to pronounce anything, more wrinkled, more firmly pressed against the fine line of lower teeth, which are even more visible with the years (one begins to bite from below)."

The poem "memory or statue" presents the vibrations of bodies trapped somewhere between stop-time and climax. It also resists the traditional aesthetic pairing of male artist and female object-model: here, the speaker gazes at Antinous, mentally caressing a motionless and nude figure of male beauty. The contemplation of the body climaxes

somewhere past sexuality, within a metanarrative about the speaker as writer: "I'll reconstruct a statue beyond a life oppressed in life, oppressed in consciousness; I'll write Fernando Pessoa's poem 'Antinous' all over again; I'll write Hadrian's memories all over again, I'll kiss you in museums and you'll wake from the dead culture in the prolonged space of representation that is your mouth, its flat lips, like a map of the excess of you."

The speaker desires Antinous' return, but her kiss cannot guarantee that he will awaken. If stop-time enables an exploration of minds and bodies, it also breathes an analytical chill. Rodríguez remarks that the book's images are less living or coming back to life than "dissected" (DSDE). In this respect, her poems invoke a cautionary tale told by her friend and fellow writer Antonio José Ponte. Ponte argues that institutionalized revolution generates an impossible project when it attempts to extend the moment of revolution itself. He begins with a reflection from Walter Benjamin's Arcades project: "Benjamin wrote that, during the Commune, the clocks on the faces of buildings were favorite targets for revolutionary sharpshooters. Practically all the public clocks in Paris ended up stopped by bullets. The gunshots of the Communards sought to stop time forever" (218). However, "time had dedicated only a moment to that triumph, as if it were nothing special," and

> the revolution in power would undertake to punish such insolence, to combat time. It would call attention over and over to that precious moment of triumph, it would make history, meaning, den-

sity in a moment. It would invent commemora-
tions, the calendar of the Revolution, a new as-
tronomy, a kingdom of self-torture and guilt: How
does one call oneself revolutionary when every-
one, sympathizers or not of the abrupt change,
innocents, accomplices and executioners, now
finds him- or herself, forever, outside the mo-
ment of the Revolution? (218)

Stop-time in *Foto* could either reproduce this failed dream
or challenge the assumption that stopping time is the only
way to live "revolution." The book explores both options,
but when interviewed, Rodríguez tends to emphasize the
failures of writing and its claims to achieve transcendence
(DSDE).

Perhaps the most compelling poem from the book, and
one which explicitly conflates revolutionary martyrdom
with that of Christ, is " — at least, that's how he looked,
backlit —." The image of Che Guevara anchors the poem.[25]
In his photograph we see

the body's reserve in a face's demeanor,
that speck of life, like the man himself,
that distant man whom I now see in the photo
something moral, something cold.

Here is the return of the "genuine moral body" of Cuban
discourse. Present in the photograph, it interwines with
imagery of Christ. The icon even reappears in a new body:
"(his son) my friend, the poet, the carpenter of the Malecón,"

who "walks in cracked sandals through / the streets of Havana." However, Rodríguez signals that the transmission of the image, its translation into other moments and bodies, has been disrupted. The speaker states, "I've exiled that reality into the past," spearing the photograph with a tack. Rather than arriving at a newly stable conviction by the end of the poem, she ends with half-statement, half-question: "You still require some faith from me?"

What *Foto* proposes is not utopia's permanence or a triumph over time. The frozen moral body of the past never truly breaks through the surface of the poem to re-occupy the present; the speaker warns against the "fictitious supposition of entering history."[26] The poet gives up her hold on the bodies, statues, and icons that might have been preserved inside it. Depicting, instead, a series of "ephemeral things" (IDGM), Rodríguez offers the freedoms of a revised vision, a revolutionary gaze that depends not on freezing the hands of time but on embracing its motion. In her poetic testimonies, it is not any single moment of triumph that gives meaning to revolution, but the everyday, intimate, and ambivalent experiences that citizens share — even if they know heroes and history only from a distance.

La azotea de Reina (Reina's Rooftop)

With *Foto*, Rodríguez won her second Casa de las Américas prize, reaffirming her prominence as a literary figure on the island. Yet she has been important in Havana's cultural scene for more than one reason. While her writing

represents one kind of struggle and innovation, her home represents another. The *azotea* has served as a space for readings and discussions in the time-honored tradition of *tertulias*, gatherings both social and intellectual; at the same time, it is a place for performing a strangely visible resistance to the revolutionary embrace of local culture. Nonetheless, family members and cats have their places here. Rodríguez' home represents a center of her energies, a place where her literary and lived struggles intersect. The space permits her work and life to exist in "intense circularity," a circularity that Rodríguez has linked back to the body, synechdochically represented by the womb.[27]

Like so many homes in Havana, Rodriguez' rooftop apartment has no doorbell. The visitor stands in the street and hollers up at the roof in an effort to get someone's attention. It's especially difficult to get Rodriguez' attention because she lives on top of a tall building. Once inside the door, the visitor enters a stairwell, dark except for whatever natural light comes through the occasional window during daylight hours. The main handrail leans drunkenly off to one side. Until Jorge Miralles, Rodríguez' partner, repainted the stairwell for the new millennium, poetry and other intellectual graffiti — years' worth of lines, verses or entire poems written across gray backgrounds in black marker and white paint — showed up on the dilapidated walls and the slanting undersides of the stairways.

Journalist Elizabeth Hanly visited Reina's rooftop in 1994. She described the community atmosphere, beginning with the origins of the salon in the 1980s: "One by one, the

younger writers — perhaps 60 — began to congregate at Reina's rooftop. Artists and writers come here to shower if there's no water, to study when there's no light at home. Havana's current austerity measures include rationed electricity in most parts of the city. By chance, Reina's house is in a section whose underground cables cannot regularly be turned on or off without damaging them permanently. When writers like Omar Pérez aren't able to read publicly anywhere else, they read on her 'patio,' a euphemism for the part of the roof that isn't her house."[28] In spite of the shortages of the Special Period, many of these young poets from the *azotea* were already seeing success, publishing internationally and winning prizes.

Madeline Cámara, also writing in 1994, described a broad cultural context for the salon: "Artistic and intellectual production continues to flourish on the island because, among other reasons, they are among the best ways of resisting the country's external and internal blockades" (729), blockades respectively levelled by the governments of the United States (through the embargo) and Cuba (through internal censorship). Noting that the Rodríguez rooftop housed one of the groups that she had in mind, Cámara added, "In literature we have seen the continuing enrichment of poetry as the genre of choice to reflect, at an individual level, on the crisis of the country and its inhabitants. This community of discourse has endured, demonstrating a desire to remain independent of official institutions which leave no doubt as to their disapproval of the oppositional cultural politics" (729-730).

For Rodríguez herself, the ultimate ideal for the rooftop was to produce work that would level hierarchies of all kinds. This ideal had at least two reasons for being important to her. It mirrored her aesthetic interests, her interest in language and transgression. It also conflated domestic and intellectual spaces, challenging gender divisions. Rodríguez addresses gender gingerly: "I needed to feel recognized in relation to a male-oriented culture. Not for the sake of being a feminist. But for the sake of being a person who tried to be there, to be there along with what was coming out or happening. And that effort exposed me to the contributions of people who had left their homes to go out searching, hunting for other contexts" (DSDE).

However, the rooftop's successes have been tempered by new challenges, a constant reminder that the private home, like creative expression, is never truly separated from public life. Intellectuals still collect on the Havana rooftop, but in smaller numbers. By 1998 Rodríguez ruefully admitted that health problems limited her ability to host the multitudes of visitors whom she had been accustomed to entertaining. But there were other reasons for the change. A Cuban familiar with the salon privately (and anonymously) pointed to disillusionment among participants. He offered one possible interpretation of the state politics which contributed to that disillusionment: the government seemed to have learned a lesson by studying what other countries did incorrectly. Permitting alternative cultural sites to exist would be a sort of safety valve for Cuba, he explained, allowing for the release of energies that might

lead to organized resistance if too tightly enclosed. However, this release was limited, artfully contained. When Hanly was in Havana in 1994, the group gathered at the rooftop was optimistic: they had just won a concession from the government allowing them to produce a publication. Their hopes for publication would dwindle as they realized that public consent from the government did not ensure quick results. The reasons for this de facto limitation on publishing remain unclear. Severe national economic shortages undoubtedly contributed: even paper had become hard to find in the Special Period, meaning that publications simply became harder to produce. Increasingly disillusioned with the lack of opportunities for publication and personal development within their country, familiar figures at the rooftop salon left the island for other parts of the world, and the government did not prohibit their exit.

Cultural life at the *azotea* has never been the same. By the late '90s, Rodríguez frequently invoked the distressing loss of these friends and colleagues, seeing in that loss a terrible challenge to literary production on the island more generally. As a poet, she felt herself losing important interlocutors, the people who pushed her to do her best work.

Another significant challenge was that of making a living. Rodríguez recalled her struggles to decide which kinds of writing were most important to her, given that she was trying to support her family: "A moment arrived when I thought that it was going to be very hard for me, because I don't write in order to sell. There's a novel that I've been writing for fourteen years. It's not about placement in a

market. That's an example of holding to a standard of quality, to work for literature, to maintain the levels that you've required for yourself. You require it from yourself, and you can survive. That's very difficult." She spoke candidly about her feeling of guilt, her sense that her needs as a writer have conflicted with those of her children, admitting, "A lot of the time, this way of life scares me. I get scared a lot. And I'm afraid that I've been wrong, I've been selfish" (IDGM).

Looking out her doorway at the open sky, Rodríguez reflected, "I like the sky at twilight . . . I like this thing I've made, this house, built piecemeal. It's what I was able to make, practically with my bare hands — there's nothing luxurious about it, but I know what kind of work went into everything. And then, I have my daughter, and my sons; my mother is alive at seventy-seven and active and still working" (IDGM). Rodríguez finally sent her novel out for consideration in 2002, still struggling with her family's material deprivations.

In the new century Rodríguez developed an additional reason to stay on the island: she co-founded *Azoteas* (*Rooftops*) with Antón Arrufat. Together they edit the magazine, with Miralles' assistance. Its title clearly references the salon hosted at Rodríguez and Miralles' home, lending a new aspect to the cultural importance of this simultaneously public and private home. Published under the auspices of the Cuban Book Institute, *Azoteas* opened with a statement about nation and cultural policy. The manifesto on the cover of the magazine's first issue proposed that

Cuba's dispersed population be recognized officially within the island's cultural institutions, meaning that cultural figures in exile should be included in the nation's cultural histories and ongoing publishing projects. The historical relevance of this argument may be appreciated when one considers complaints lodged earlier from outside the island, such as Ileana Fuentes-Perez' observations in *Outside Cuba / Fuera de Cuba: Contemporary Cuban Visual Artists / Artistas Cubanos Contemporáneos* (1989). Fuentes-Perez documents shifts in Cuba's laws about artistic expression and national policy. She critiques both laws and less obvious silencing mechanisms. Focusing on the omission of exiled artists from the island's histories and educational campaigns, she writes, "The State gives artists their prominence, and also erases them." Many renowned artists "have been removed from public view, and are inaccessible, as a result of their exile" (24-5). The manifesto published by Rodríguez and Arrufat in *Azoteas* 1 responds to such observations about the island's official cultural genealogy by challenging erasures: "Cuban writers and artists are dispersed: when two of them in Mexico City or in Madrid, in Miami or in Havana, refer to a third and absent person, they give that person life. Cuban culture will not be able to limit itself to the figure on the island."[29] In keeping with the manifesto, *Azoteas* has published work by writers now living outside the island, like José Kozer (a resident of Florida).[30]

In addition to taking up editorial work with *Azoteas*, Rodríguez became involved in another organization that,

like the Book Institute, is housed in Old Havana's centrally located Palacio del Segundo Cabo. The Casa de Letras sits atop the impressive colonial palace, overlooking the Plaza de Armas. It houses a growing library and serves as a site for workshops promoting writing and translation. Reflecting on her involvement with the library and workshops, Rodríguez commented that she has occasionally been able to suppress her need to socialize with other artists and writers but has never eliminated it entirely. If these community activities consume time that could be used for writing, they also renew the dialogues that Rodríguez requires for continued growth as a writer.

Today, writes Davies, Rodríguez has achieved prominence: "About a dozen women poets born between 1940 and 1960, usually referred to as the poets of the Revolution, have published continuously throughout the post-1959 period. The most famous internationally is Nancy Morejón; the poet who perhaps commands the greatest respect in Cuba is Reina María Rodríguez" (125). Surprisingly, it's hard to find Rodríguez' books of poetry in Cuban bookstores. Economic pressures continue to restrict state publishing activity. Even those of her books that won the first Casa de las Américas title and the Julián del Casal prizes are not to be found in stores. Rodríguez herself does not have any copies left, having given them away to friends and admirers. Fortunately, she has access to a computer, where she keeps material on disk. It is one of those disks full of poetry that we have translated here, hoping to put her work back into print in two languages.

★

This project could not have been completed without support from colleagues, institutions, and family. First and foremost, the translators thank Reina María Rodríguez for her participation in this project. We also acknowledge many other people who have facilitated this project when practical difficulties could have impeded it. Without Jorge Guitart's careful readings and sound advice, this project would have been impossible. We thank Eugenio Rodríguez and José Buscaglia-Salgado for their assistance both in Havana and in the United States. Thanks are also due to Ricardo Gutiérrez Mouat at Emory University for his early encouragement, good counsel, and continued assistance; and to Arnaldo Valero of the Gonzalo Picón Febre Institute of Literary Research in Mérida, Venezuela, for bringing our attention to Reina María Rodríguez' work in the first place. Susan Kalter, Deborah Meadows, and Jim Pancrazio gave helpful commentary on the Afterword. We recognize Nydia Roque, who indirectly provided us with our first introductions to Cuba, for her years of work as a teacher. The Department of English and the College of Arts and Sciences at Illinois State University supported in part the production of this book. The Latin American, Caribbean, and Iberian Studies Program at the University of Wisconsin at Madison generously provided grant money for travel to Cuba. Support from Charles Bernstein, Robert Creeley, and Dennis Tedlock through the Gray, Capen, and McNulty Chairs at the State University of New York at Buffalo made

possible a series of readings, discussions, and travels that greatly enriched this project.

Selected translations from this anthology appear in *boundary 2: An International Journal of Literature and Culture* 29:3 (Duke UP, 2002); *Mandorla: New Writing from the Americas / Nueva escritura de las Américas* 7; *A.BACUS* 148, "Culture Deceased: The Poetry of Reina María Rodríguez" (Potes & Poets Press, 2002); *Hopscotch: A Cultural Review* 2:2 (Duke UP, 2000); and *Zazil* 1 (Factory School, 2000).

[1] "Desire for Something that Doesn't Exist," hereafter DSDE.

[2] Schwartz, commenting on Lacanian interpretations of language. "Introduction."

[3] Ibid.

[4] "Las islas / the islands."

[5] Poet, journalist, essayist and patriot José Martí, who died in a battle for Cuban independence at the end of the nineteenth century.

[6] Bianchi Rosas, "Cara a cara con Reina María Rodríguez."

[7] In addition to major novels such as *The Lost Steps* and *Explosion in a Cathedral*, Carpentier is known for his construction of "the marvelous real" as a cultural vision specific to the Americas.

[8] Bejel 344.

[9] Here it must be noted that scholars of Cuban culture frequently characterize local concerns and traditions not as "pure" or "isolated" practices but as cosmopolitan in history and current practice — that is, the "local" never relin-

quishes engagement with work from the outside. Incessant exchanges disrupt the potential isolation of the island.

[10] Saldívar 15.

[11] "Declaración de la UNEAC acerca de los premios otorgados a Heberto Padilla en Poesía y Antón Arrufat en Teatro. 15 de noviembre de 1968." In the 1998 Ediciones Universal edition of *Fuera del juego*, 120. My translation.

[12] For a more detailed discussion of the Padilla affair, see the above-mentioned Ediciones Universal *Fuera del juego*. This volume includes accompanying documents, such as Padilla's 1967 article in the magazine *Caimán barbudo*, which was interpreted as being counterrevolutionary; a transcript of Padilla's self-criticism; and letters from prominent intellectuals outside Cuba responding to Padilla's imprisonment.

[13] While there is not space to pursue this topic in detail in this essay, Navarro discusses further details of Cuba's complex shifts in cultural policy and the public image of the intellectual at some length. See "In Medias Res Publicas."

[14] Interview with Kristin Dykstra and Nancy Gates-Madsen, 1998, hereafter IDGM.

[15] Rodríguez decided not to publish another collection of poetry — one completed after *La gente de mi barrio* and prior to *Cuando una mujer no duerme* — even though it had received an award from UNEAC.

[16] Bejel 347.

[17] Interview with Rosa Alcalá and Kristin Dykstra, 2001.

[18] Dominguez 47.

[19] *"La rue de mauvaises herbes."*

[20] "Alguna vez. algún tiempo" / "on some occasion. at some time."

[21] *La rue de mauvaises herbes.*

[22] Published in *Mandorla: New Writing from the Americas* 4. Reprinted with the permission of Roberto Tejada.

[23] IDGM. Rodríguez does not recall the name of the story that she read before composing "Violet Island."

[24] See Valdés, esp. 212-213.

[25] When I first received this poem in an email, Rodríguez had saved the file as "Che.doc." This inspired both earnest and strange thoughts about the electronic transmission of the revolutionary icon.

[26] "Memory or statue."

[27] "Intense Circularity."

[28] "Revolutionary Fight for Poetic Licence."

[29] Rodríguez has also spoken of an attempt to confront histories of exile and cultural suppression directly by seeking an invitation for Heberto Padilla to return to the island and read his work. However, Padilla passed away before arrangements could be completed. Meanwhile, Cuban-American writers and artists in the United States have themselves made imaginative runs on the embargo; a few prominent examples include Coco Fusco, Achy Obejas, and Cristina García.

[30] Kozer became the first Cuban-American to have a book of poems published on the island and has since been included in such publications as *Unión: Revista de literatura y arte* 47 (UNEAC, July-Sept. 2002).

Works Cited

Bejel, Emilio. "Reina María Rodríguez." *Escribir en Cuba. Entrevistas con escritores cubanos: 1979-1989*. Río Piedras: Editorial de la Universidad de Puerto Rico, 1991. 343-356.

Beverly, John, ed. *boundary 2: An International Journal of Literature and Culture* 29.3 (Fall 2002): 1-11.

Bianchi Rosas, Ciro. "Cara a cara con Reina María Rodríguez." *Cuba Internacional* 179 (octubre 1984): 72-74.

Cámara, Madeleine. "Third Options: Beyond the Border." *Michigan Quarterly Review Special Issue: Bridges to Cuba/ Puentes a Cuba* (Fall 1994): 723-731.

Davies, Catherine. *A Place in the Sun? Women Writers in Twentieth-Century Cuba*. London: Zed Books, 1997.

Dominguez, Jorge. "Cuba since 1959." *Cuba: A Short History* (1993). Ed. Leslie Bethell. NY: Cambridge UP, 1998 (reprint). 95-148.

Fuentes-Pérez, Ileana. "By Choice or by Circumstance: The Inevitable Exile of Artists." *Outside Cuba / Fuera de Cuba: Contemporary Cuban Visual Artists / Artistas Cubanos Contemporáneos*. New Brunswick, N.J.: Office of Hispanic Arts, Mason Gross School of the Arts, Rutgers State University of New Jersey; Miami, Fla.: Research Institute for Cuban Studies, University of Miami, 1989.

Hanly, Elizabeth. "Revolutionary Fight for Poetic Licence." The Guardian 25:1, 13 August 1994: 2.

Muguercia, Magaly. "The Body and its Politics in Cuba of the Nineties" (2000). Beverley 175-185.

Navarro, Desiderio. "In Medias Res Publicas: On Intellec-

tuals and Social Criticism in the Cuban Public Sphere." Tr. Alessandro Fornazzari and Desiderio Navarro. Beverley 187-203.

Padilla, Heberto. *Fuera del juego*. Ed. conmemorativa, 1968-1998; 1. ed. conmemorativa. Miami, Fla.: Ediciones Universal, 1998.

Ponte, Antonio José. "The Supervised Party." Beverley 215-224.

Plural: Revista cultural de Excelsior 234, Vol. 26, 2nda época (marzo 1991): 4-17.

Rodríguez, Reina María. "'Desire for Something that Doesn't Exist': Interview between Reina María Rodríguez and Kristin Dykstra." *HOW* 2 Vol. I No. 7 (Spring 2002). Archived at <http://www.departments.bucknell.edu/stadler_center/how2/>.

—————————. *En la arena de Padua*. Ciudad de la Habana: Ediciones Unión, 1992.

—————————. "Intense Circularity: From the Uterus, to the Rooftop, to the Reading." Interview with Rosa Alcalá. *A.BACUS* #148 (15 August 2002).

—————————. *La foto del invernadero*. El Vedado, La Habana: Casa de las Américas, 1998.

—————————. Interview with Rosa Alcalá and Kristin Dykstra. Havana: 11 and 24 June 2001.

—————————. Interview with Kristin Dykstra and Nancy Gates Madsen. Havana: 30 July 1998.

—————————. *Para un cordero blanco*. Ciudad de la Habana: Casa de las Américas, 1984.

—————————. *Páramos*. Ciudad de la Habana:

Ediciones Unión, 1995.

Saldívar, José David. *The Dialectics of Our America: Genealogy, Cultural Critique, and Literary History*. Durham: Duke UP, 1991.

Schwartz, Leonard. "Introduction: Impossibility of / Necessity of / Speech." *A.BACUS* #150 (15 November 2002).

Valdés, Nelson. "Cuban Political Culture: Between Betrayal and Death." *Cuba in Transition: Crisis and Transformation*. Ed. Sandor Halebsky and John M. Kirk. San Francisco: Westview Press, 1992. 207-228.

GREEN INTEGER
Pataphysics and Pedantry

Douglas Messerli, *Publisher*

Essays, Manifestos, Statements, Speeches, Maxims,
Epistles, Diaristic Notes, Narratives, Natural Histories,
Poems, Plays, Performances, Ramblings, Revelations
and all such ephemera as may appear necessary
to bring society into a slight tremolo of confusion
and fright at least.

*

THE MARJORIE G. PERLOFF SERIES
OF INTERNATIONAL POETRY

This series is published in honor of Marjorie G. Perloff
and her contributions, past and present,
to the literary criticism of international poetry
and poetics. Perloff's writing and teaching have been
illuminating and broad-reaching,
affecting even the publisher of Green Interger;
for without her influence and friendship,
he might never have engaged in publishing poetry.

2002

Yang Lian *Yi* (GI 35) [China]
Lyn Hejinian *My Life* (GI 39) [USA]
Else Lasker-Schüler *Selected Poems* (GI 49) [Germany]
Gertrude Stein *Tender Buttons* (GI 50) [USA]
Hagiwara Sakutarō *Howling at the Moon:*
Poems and Prose (GI 57) [Japan]

2003

Rainer Maria Rilke *Duino Elegies* (GI 58) [Germany]
Paul Celan *Romanian Poems* (GI 81) [Romania]
Adonis *If Only the Sea Could Sleep* (GI 84) [Syria/Lebanon]
Henrik Nordbrandt *The Hangman's Lament* (GI 95)
[Denmark]
Mario Luzi *Earthly and Heavenly Journey*
of Simone Martini (GI 99) [Italy]

2004

André Breton *Earthlight* (GI 102) [France]
Paul Celan *Breathturn* (GI 111) [Bukovina/France]
Paul Celan *Threadsuns* (GI 112) [Bukovina/France]
Paul Celan *Lightduress* (GI 113) [Bukovina/France]
Reina María Rodríguez *Violet Island and Other Poems*
(GI 119) [Cuba]
Amelia Rosselli *War Variations* (GI 121) [Italy]

FROM OUR BACKLIST